Rudolph S. Spreckels

with the respects of

Robt. H. [illegible]

NORTH DUTCH CHURCH.

A

HISTORICAL DISCOURSE

ON THE

Reformed Prot. Dutch Church of Albany,

DELIVERED ON

THANKSGIVING DAY, NOVEMBER 26, 1857,

IN

THE NORTH DUTCH CHURCH,

BY THE PASTOR,

REV. E. P. ROGERS, D. D.

PUBLISHED BY REQUEST OF CONSISTORY.

NEW YORK:
BOARD OF PUBLICATION
OF THE
REFORMED PROTESTANT DUTCH CHURCH.
337 BROADWAY.
1858.

MUNSELL, PRINTER, ALBANY.

HISTORICAL DISCOURSE.

Walk about Zion, and go round about her; tell the towers thereof. Mark ye well her bulwarks, consider her palaces; that ye may tell it to the generation following.—PSALM xlviii: 12, 13.

Thus does the pious psalmist exhort us to note with zealous care, the history and character of the Church of God. To trace out that history, to record her progress, to take note of God's dealings with her from time to time, and testify to her advancement and triumph, is a grateful task, and a solemn duty. Especially when that history runs over the track of centuries, should this duty be discharged. For as the river widens its channel, and bears richer freight on its bosom, as it flows farther and faster from its source, so as we follow the history of the Church down the stream of time, we find it richer in interest, and more deeply laden with the treasures of the Divine presence and blessing.

And what is true of the church at large, is no less true of individual churches and congregations. We regard it as the solemn duty of every church to keep a faithful record of its history, and to afford the opportunity to succeeding generations to know something of its origin, its progress, its vicissitudes, its foes, its struggles and its triumphs. The ancient Jews were required "to instruct their children that they might convey throughout all generations the history of those Divine interpositions and mercies with which they had been favored." And the obligation is no less binding upon Christian churches, thus to keep in perpetual remembrance the dealings of God with them for the information and encouragement of succeeding generations.

Impelled by such considerations, I have undertaken to prepare in a concise and summary form, a sketch of the history of the Reformed Protestant Dutch Church of Albany, being the Church with which we are happily connected in our several relations as pastor, officers, families and communicants. I have sought to make this brief, but comprehensive, including all the main facts in our history, so far as they could be gathered from accessible sources, but going slightly into details which would swell the sketch into dimensions utterly beyond the limits afforded by the present occasion.

Before proceeding, however, to the history, let us notice for a moment the name and the origin of the Church to which we belong. Our name is "THE REFORMED PROTESTANT DUTCH CHURCH OF ALBANY." We are the PROTESTANT Dutch Church, because we are descended from those in the sixteenth century, who boldly *protested* against the authority of the pope, and the false and unscriptural tenets and practices of the Church of Rome. We are the REFORMED Protestant Dutch Church because we are of those who differed from some of the early Protestants, and from Luther himself, on some points, particularly in respect to the presence of the humanity of Christ in the Holy Supper. We are the Reformed Protestant DUTCH Church, because we are descended from that branch of the Reformed Church which was organized in Holland. Our doctrinal standards and polity are derived primarily from the action of those who met at Antwerp in 1563, "and adopted a system of principles and rules which laid the foundation, and in a great measure formed the full texture of church government and order adopted by subsequent synods."

We bear a name, every word of which is connected with the grandest historical associations and the noblest memories of the past. It associates us with some of the brightest names in the catalogue of God's illustrious servants. It dates back more than three hundred years, to the day when six princes of the German empire made their manly protest against the decrees of the Diet of Spires, and associates us with that glorious era, when, at the command of God, light, the light of the Reformation, illumined the dark ages and brought freedom to imprisoned souls. It connects us with such illustrious names as Wessel Gansevoort and Rudolf Agricola;* as Luther, Calvin, Zuinglius, Knox, Cranmer and others, who labored with zeal and devotion in the cause of God's truth in Germany, Switzerland, France, the Netherlands, Scotland and England. And it connects us with that land which was first redeemed from the jaws of the sea by the energy and industry of its inhabitants, and afterwards became the centre of commerce, the mistress of the seas, and the arena for the noblest exhi-

* See Appendix, Note A.

bitions of pure patriotism, heroic courage, sublime fortitude and martyr devotion to the right which the world has ever witnessed. Our Mother Church was distinguished in that day for the profound learning of her theologians, the devotion of her pastors, the purity of her creed, and the scriptural beauty of her forms of worship. She opened her arms freely to welcome the fugitive Huguenot, the outlawed Jew, and the exiled Puritan. She sheltered in her bosom the wanderer from the valleys of Piedmont, and the mountains of Scotland. She had drank of the bitter cup of persecution, and the sufferer for conscience sake, though a stranger to her land and her dialect, was ever hailed as a brother in their common Lord. It is needless to speak of the learning of her scholars, the genius of her artists, the prowess of her warriors. They have all hewed out for themselves enduring niches in the Temple of Fame.

Such are the associations and the memories connected with our name and origin. And it is worthy of notice, that those noble men who landed on Plymouth Rock, and to whom this western world owes so much, came from their own land by way of the land of your fathers, where for twelve years they found a safe retreat from persecution, and enjoyed the Christian hospitality of their Dutch brethren. That twelve years of sojourn in the Netherlands might have been no unimportant portion of the training of the Pilgrims, for the work which lay before them on the rocky shores of New England.

In the autumn of 1609, Hendrik Hudson anchored his little vessel in the river which bears his name, opposite the bank on which now stands the city of Albany. In 1614, six years before the landing of the Mayflower at Plymouth, trading posts were established here and at New York, then Fort Orange and Manhattan. The first permanent agricultural colony was established in New Netherlands in 1623. In 1630, a tract of land around Fort Orange was purchased by Kilian Van Rensselaer, and a colony was at once planted here of which he was the head, or patroon. Kilian Van Rensselaer, was a merchant of Amsterdam, a dealer in pearls, and a director in the Dutch West India Company. The tract purchased by him of the Indians was twenty-four miles long and forty-eight broad; containing over 700,000 acres of land, lying now in Albany, Rensselaer and

Columbia counties. This gentleman seems to have regarded the institutions of religion as a very essential element of prosperity for his colony, and his first efforts were directed towards their establishment and support. In the year 1642, he secured the services of the Rev. Johannes Megapolensis, who was at that time the pastor of two congregations in Holland, and in good repute as a man of learning and piety. The call which was sent to Domine Megapolensis, states that "By the state of navigation in the East and West Indies a door is opened through the special providence of God, also in New Netherlands for the preaching of the Gospel of Jesus Christ, for the salvation of men, as good fruits have been already witnessed there through God's mercy."* It was signed by the president and scribe of the Classis of Amsterdam, in Classical Assembly at Amsterdam, March 22d, 1642.

The salary which the domine was to receive for the six years of pastoral labor which was stipulated, was 1100 guilders ($440), 22½ bushels of wheat, and 2 firkins of butter per annum for the first three years, and if his labors

* See Appendix, Note B.

were satisfactory to the patroon, he was to receive an additional amount of 200 guilders ($80), per annum for the succeeding three years. In addition to this he was to receive $120, by way of outfit, and a free passage and board for himself and family to his new field of labor. A house was also to be provided for him on his arrival at Rensselaerswyck. It was also stipulated that in case he was captured by the Dunkirkers on the passage, measures were to be taken immediately for his ransom, and a certain sum allowed monthly for his support. In case of his death before the expiration of the six years, provision was to be made for the support of his family till the end of that term. These provisions may be called just and liberal, and they show conclusively that the then head of the colony duly estimated the value of the institutions of religion, and the services of a pious and learned ministry.

Having accepted this call, Domine Megapolensis embarked for this country with his wife and four children, of whom the oldest was fourteen and the youngest eight years of age, and arrived on the 11th of August 1642. He was then in the thirty-ninth year of his age, and consequently was just in his prime. His character while a minister in Holland was that of "a good, honest, and pure preacher." In the call from the Classis of Amsterdam he is styled "a faithful servant of the Gospel of the Lord." He must have been a man of zeal and devotion of more than ordinary character, to have been willing to leave a sphere of usefulness and honor in his native land, for the perils of the sea and the toils and privations incident to a new and savage country. No attractive prospect of ease or honor awaited him, on the banks of the far distant Hudson. A small colony in an unknown land, in the midst of savages, and subject to all the perils and discomforts of pioneer life, was to be his field of labor. Yet we find him ready at the call of his classis to break the ties which bound him to his native land; to part from two churches with whom he was happily connected, and with a spirit worthy of a true Hollander, to come, the apostle of a pure Christianity, to these western shores.

Domine Megapolensis remained during the six years of his agreement, faithfully discharging the duties of his office. He not only labored among the colonists, but took a great interest in preaching to the Indians. Numbers of these resorted to Fort Orange for the purposes of trade, and the domine learned their language, and preached the Gospel to them, several years before the celebrated Eliot began his labors among the Indians in New England. He was the author of a treatise on the Mohawks, which was afterwards published in Holland. His efforts among them were crowned with much success. At a later date the names of many baptized Indians are found in the early records of the Church, the fruits of the labors begun by the worthy domine who was its first pastor, and the first missionary to the red men of the forest.*

His term of service having expired, Dr. Megapolensis left the colony to return to the fatherland. On his arrival at New Amsterdam (now New York) he was prevailed on by Gov. Stuyvesant to remain there in place of Domine Backerus, who had returned to Holland. The representations of the governor, of the spiritual destitution prevailing in New Amsterdam had such weight with the domine, that he consented to remain, and labored more than twenty years as senior pastor, being assisted from 1664 to 1668 by his son Samuel, who was educated

* See Appendix, Note C.

both in divinity and medicine, and who returned to Holland a short time before his father's death, which occured in 1670, in the sixty-seventh year of his age.

The first house of worship in Albany, was built on the arrival of Dr. Megapolensis. It stood near the fort, in what is now called Church street. It was a plain wooden building, thirty-four feet long by nineteen wide, furnished with a pulpit ornamented with a canopy, pews for the magistrates and church officers, and nine benches for the people. In this simple structure the congregation worshiped thirteen years.

The second minister of the Church at Albany was the Rev. Gideon Schaats. He was born in 1607, and was at first a schoolmaster in Holland. Having received ordination, he was sent to this country in 1652, in company with the Rev. Samuel Drisius, a man of great learning, who was able to preach in Dutch, English and French, and who became a colleague of Dr. Megapolensis at New Amsterdam. Dominie Schaats was forty-five years of age when he arrived in this country, and he labored here for more than thirty years. He died in a good old age leaving three children, the eldest of whom, a son, was killed at the great massacre in Schenectady, Feb. 10, 1690. His remaining children, a son and married daughter, are supposed to have outlived their father many years. The house in which Domine Schaats resided, stood on the north-east corner of North Pearl and State streets. It is said to have been imported from Holland, bricks, wood-work, tiles, and ornamental irons with which it was profusely adorned, expressly for his use, in the same vessel which brought over the pulpit and the bell, for the new Church. It stood from 1657 to 1832, and was for some time the residence of Balthazar Lydius, a grandson of Domine Lydius, who died in 1815, aged 78 years.

Four years after the settlement of Mr. Schaats the congregation erected their second house of worship. It was built at the intersection of what is now State street with Broadway. It is supposed by some that this building was of stone, but we find that in 1714 a petition was addressed to Governor Hunter, then governor in chief of the province of New York, which purports to be "The humble petition of Petrus Van Driesen, Minister of the Nether Dutch Reformed Congregation of the city and county of

Albany, and the Elders and Deacons of the said Congregation," which states in substance that the Church which was built in 1656, "being built of timber and boards, is by time so much decayed that they find themselves under necessity of building a new one in its place," and concludes by praying his excellency "to approve and encourage this pious work."*

It would appear from this that the building was of wood. The corner stone was laid by Rutger Jacobsen, one of the magistrates of the city, and the ancestor of the venerable lady, now a member of this Church, who has become distinguished by her munificent patronage of astronomical science.† As this was an edifice intended to last for many years, the congregation determined that the pulpit should come from the same noble land, from which its occupants were imported. So they sent to Holland for an oaken pulpit and a bell, both of which in due season arrived, and were erected in their appropriate places. The old pulpit, after having been occupied for a period of one hundred and fifty years by a succession of able and faithful pastors, is still preserved in this

* See Appendix, Note D. † Mrs. Blandina Dudley.

edifice, a fine specimen of architectural proportions and workmanship, and an interesting and valuable memorial of the past.

In 1675 we find that the Rev. Mr. Niewenhuysen (or Niewenhuyt) was a colleague with Mr. Schaats, but I have not been able to learn any particulars of his history. During his ministry Rev. Nicholas Van Renssalaer (or Ranslaer) arrived in Albany, and set up a claim to the pulpit, and also to the manor: neither of which claims were successful. He was not approved by the Classis of Amsterdam, and was moreover strongly suspected of being a papist in disguise. He however had the governor on his side, Sir Edmund Andross, to whom he had been recommended by the Duke of York, and who endeavored to obtain for him a living in the Church. Mr. Niewenhuysen stoutly resisted this attempt, and suffered much oppressive treatment in consequence, at the governor's hands. The people however sympathized with him and refused to acknowledge Mr. Van Renssalaer as a minister, or admit his claims to any consideration from his clerical character.

In 1683 the Rev. Godfreidus Dellius, was

PULPIT OF THE OLD CHURCH,

Built in Holland, 1656.

sent out as assistant to Domine Schaats, who was now upwards of seventy-five years of age. There are no church records prior to this date extant in any connected form, but in this year the Register of Baptism begins, which has continued to be kept with much accuracy down to the present day. Mr. Dellius found the Church large and flourishing. It contained among its catechumens and its communicants some of the Indians in the vicinity, and large additions were made during the sixteen years of his ministry. It is said that the baptisms during this period reached the astonishing number of eleven hundred. The list of members in 1683, in the hand writing of Mr. Dellius, amounts to between six and seven hundred. It is interesting in looking over this list to notice how many of the names still are found among the present members, having come down in unbroken succession from the godly men and women of two hundred years ago.*

At a meeting of the magistrates of the town, holden August 13th, 1683, the following resolutions were adopted:

"Resolved, That a letter be written to the Venerable, Pious, and very Learned the Minis-

* See Appendix, Note E.

ters and members of the very Rev. the Classis of Amsterdam, assembled at Amsterdam, sincerely thanking their Rev. for their Fatherly care, in sending over the Rev. Pious and Learned Dom. Goddefridus Dellius, with whom the congregation is highly pleased.

"Resolved, Also to write to Sieur Richard Van Renssalaer and Sieur Abel D'Wollff to thank them heartily for the trouble they have taken, in finding out the Rev. Pious and Learned Dom. Goddefridus Dellius, who arrived here on the 2d inst. to the great joy of every one, and whose preaching was heard with the greatest satisfaction and contentment."

Mr. Dellius remained with the Church for a period of sixteen years, and sailed for Holland in 1699.

In 1699, Dominie Johannes Petrus Nucella, began his labors, which continued only three or four years. The date of the first baptisms administered by him is Sept. 3d, 1699. During his ministry the rite of baptism was administered as far down the river as Kinderhook, as the sacrament of the Lord's supper had been administered by his predecessor at Schenectady four times a year. Very little is known of the peculiar character of Mr. Nucella, or of the results of his ministry in Albany. His connection with the congregation seems to have terminated in 1702.

The next minister was the Rev. Johannes Lydius, who commenced his labors in 1703. Like his predecessors, Domine Lydius seems to have interested himself much in the instruction and conversion of the Indians. There is mention made of his having labored among the tribes of the Five Nations, and of his receiving from the governor and council pecuniary compensation for such labors. He died on the 1st day of March, 1710. In a letter written by the Rev. Thomas Barclay, an Episcopal minister at Albany in that year, to the secretary of "the Society for the propagation of the Gospel in foreign parts," he mentions Domine Lydius in terms of high commendation, speaking of him as an intimate friend, and fellow laborer, and mentioning that by his death the Dutch Church and about thirty Indian communicants have been left without a pastor. Domine Lydius left a son, John Henry Lydius, a prominent Indian trader in the colony of New York, who retired to England in 1776, and died at

Kensington near London in 1791, in the ninety-eighth year of his age.*

After the death of Domine Lydius, the Church continued without a pastor for about two years. During this time, however, they were not entirely destitute of the preaching of the word, or the administration of the sacraments. The Rev. Gualterus Du Bois, who was a minister in the Church in New York for fifty-one years, and who is described as a man of high character, and greatly beloved by his people, visited Albany in 1710, and preached and administered the sacraments. Also the Rev. Petrus Vas, who died at Kingston, performed ministerial labors here in 1711. The names of both these ministers are found on the Register of Baptisms of the above dates.

In 1712 the Rev. Petrus Van Driessen was called to the pastoral charge of the congregation. During his ministry a new edifice was built for the use of the Church, which is well remembered by some of the older members of this congregation. It was built of stone with a steep, pyramidal roof, and belfry surmounted with a weathercock, and was for its day quite

* Doc. His. of New York, Vol. III, p. 893.

OLD DUTCH CHURCH ON STATE STREET.

an imposing edifice. It was built around the old Church, which was taken down and carried out piecemeal after the walls of the new building were raised and covered. It is said that the services of public worship were interrupted only three sabbaths by reason of this removal. The new Church was of massive architecture, and solid workmanship. Each of its windows contained the coat of arms of some one of the families of the congregation, in stained glass. Several of these are still preserved, and one especially may be seen in excellent preservation at the residence of Mrs. Dudley. The seats around the walls were occupied by the respectable old burghers, the heads of families, among whom were some whose names have been distinguished in the history of the state. On the west side, were the seats occupied by the governor and the magistrates of the city. On the right and left of the pulpit, were the members of the consistory; conspicuous among them was the *voorlezer* or clerk, a very important functionary, who opened the services of the sabbath by the reading of a few texts of Scripture, the ten commandments, another chapter of the Bible, and the singing of a Psalm, the number of which was displayed on a tablet hung at the side of the pulpit, in sight of the congregation. The seats in the body of the house were occupied by the females, and the large galleries, which extended on three sides of the edifice, were appropriated to the younger male members of the congregation. It was the custom in those days for the minister to enter during the singing, and before ascending to the pulpit to stand a moment at the foot of the stairs in silent prayer, a custom which was certainly highly appropriate. In front of the desk of the pulpit was placed the hour glass, and our fathers would hardly have thought that the domine gave them good measure if he closed his discourse till the last sands had fallen. It is not often in these days that our hearers complain of the brevity of our discourses.

For ninety-one years the old stone Church stood as the centre of devotion, and place of worship for the Church of Christ in Albany. There your pious parents loved to go to worship God in simplicity and godly sincerity. There they listened with reverent attention to the preaching of the Word. There they sat down at the sacramental table, and commemorated the love of their blessed Saviour. There they carried their children to receive the rite of baptism in the name of the adorable Trinity. From that temple they were called to the purer and nobler worship of heaven. Fifty-one years have rolled away since that old building was taken down. There are but few left who were familiar with the venerable and time honored structure. It is fast becoming only a thing of tradition. Very soon the last of the smiling babes, who received baptism at its font, will be borne a gray haired man, to the silent grave. But, the results of what transpired within its walls for nearly a century, will last as long as the eternal throne of God endures.

During the ministry of Mr. Van Driessen, a petition was presented to the Hon. Peter Schuyler, president, and the rest of his majesty's council of the province of New York, for an act of incorporation. The petition is dated 3d day of August, 1720, and is signed by Petrus Van Driessen, minister; Johannes Cuyler, Johannes Roseboom, Hendrik Van Rensselaer and William Jacobse Van Deusen, elders; and Rutgert Bleecker, Volkert Van Veghten, Myndert Roseboom and Dirk Ten Broek, deacons of the Reformed Protestant Dutch Congregation in the city of Albany.*

* See Appendix, Note F.

The petition was successful, and an act of incorporation was granted to the Church under the title of the "Minister, Elders and Deacons of the Reformed Protestant Dutch Church in the city of Albany," bearing date August 10th, 1720.

Mr. Van Driessen continued in the pastoral charge of the congregation till his death, which occurred about February 1st, 1738, having labored with zeal and fidelity for a period of twenty-six years. The Church at Kinderhook was organized by him in 1712, and the Church at Claverack in 1716.

In 1733, five years prior to the death of Domine Van Driessen, the Rev. Cornelius Van Schie was settled as his colleague. Mr. Van Schie had previously labored in Poughkeepsie and Fishkill. He survived his colleague but six years, and died August 15th, 1744, aged 41 years. His last sermon was from Rev. ii, 10: "Be thou faithful unto death, and I will give thee a crown of life."

The next pastor was the Rev. Theodorus Frelinghuysen. He entered upon his labors about 1745. He was the son of the Rev. Jacobus Theodorus Frelinghuysen, a native of West Friesland, who came to this country in 1720,

Copied from the Original in possession of the Wendell Family.

Copied from Windows of the Old Church built in 1656, now in possession of the Van Rensselaer & Dudley Families.

and settled in New Jersey about three miles west of New Brunswick. He was a man of sound evangelical views, and a bold and earnest preacher. He had five sons, all of whom became ministers; and two daughters, both of whom became the wives of ministers. His second son, Johannes, succeeded his father at Raritan, in 1750, but died in 1754, in the 28th year of his age. He was the grandfather of the Hon. Theodore Frelinghuysen, president of Rutgers College. His oldest son, Theodorus, was the pastor of the Church at Albany. He is said to have been a man of more than ordinary excellence. His temper was ardent and his manners frank and popular. In the pulpit his preaching was earnest and eloquent, while his pure and spotless life, when out of it, illustrated and enforced his teachings. For fifteen years he labored beloved and respected by all, and probably no pastor was ever more deeply seated in the confidence and affections of his flock.

About this time, a regiment of royal troops was stationed in Albany, whose gay and youthful officers introduced quite a new order of things into the staid and quiet circles of the city. Parties, balls, and theatrical entertainments kept the families of the honest burghers in a continual state of flutter and excitement. The good domine in all sincerity, but perhaps in not the most judicious manner, took the field against these seductive innovations. He admonished, he preached, he prophesied, he even denounced, but with all his authority and eloquence and goodness combined, he could not exorcise from the community the rampant spirit of gaiety and fashion. There is a tradition that after having preached an unusually earnest sermon against the follies and fashions of the day, the good domine found at his door on the following Monday morning, a pair of shoes, a staff, a silver dollar and a loaf of bread. He conceived that this was an intimation that he was desired to depart, and determined at once to leave. However this may be, it is quite probable, that supposing that his influence was decidedly weakened, and being a man of peculiar sensitiveness, he withdrew from his charge, and with a grieved and humbled spirit took passage for Holland, in 1760, to visit his native land, and return again to the scene of his labors. He however never returned, and is said to have been lost overboard on the passage. A mystery hangs over his real fate, but the good people of Albany long mourned his departure and cherished his memory with the deepest affection.

Domine Frelinghuysen was succeeded in the pastoral office by the Rev. Eilardus Westerlo, a name connected with many interesting and tender associations in the history of this Church. He was born in the city of Groningen, in October, 1738. His father, Isaac Westerlo, was pastor of the Church at that place. He was named after his maternal grandfather, Eilardus Reiners, who was also a clergyman and pastor of the Church at Dalen, a village in the province of Drenthe. He was designed by his parents from his early youth for the ministry of the Gospel, and having spent six years in the Latin school at Oldenzaal, he was admitted in his 16th year to the University at Groningen, where he remained also six years, and prepared himself for examination and admission to the holy office of the ministry.

It was just at this time, when he was but twenty-two years of age, that a call from this Church was most unexpectedly placed in his hands. After due deliberation, and with the earnest advice of his instructors at the university, he decided to accept it. He was accordingly examined and approved, and in March, 1760, was installed in Holland as minister of this Church. He arrived here and entered upon his duties in the autumn of that year, and soon had reason to believe, that in removing to this city he had chosen the path of duty.

Dr. Westerlo was a man of more than ordinary religious feeling. About eight years after the commencement of his labors, he fell into a state of great despondency and fear as to his personal hopes. After a time of severe self-examination and earnest prayer, he obtained renewed hope and peace. He always considered himself to have undergone a great change at this time, and frequently spoke of it as a most interesting and eventful period of his life. He was on very intimate and friendly terms with several distinguished ministers and private Christians, and derived much edification and enjoyment from correspondence and fellowship with them. Among these were the Rev. Drs. Livingston, Laidlie, Rodgers and Mason, of New York; and Dr. Meyer, pastor of the Church at Esopus, and afterward of New Jersey; also Mrs. Livingston, mother of the late Chancellor Livingston, and other pious individuals in humbler life.

In 1775 he was married to the widow of Stephen Van Rensselaer, then Patroon of the Manor of Renssalaerswyck. She had three sons, Stephen, whose memory is still precious in this Church and city; Philip, who was for seventeen years mayor of Albany; and Elizabeth, who married for her first husband, John, a son of Gen. Philip Schuyler, and afterwards the late John Bleecker. From the time of his marriage till 1784, he resided at the Manor House. At that time he removed to the parsonage which stood in Broadway, on the site now occupied by the building known as Bleecker Hall.

Dr. Westerlo was decidedly in favor of dissolving the ecclesiastical connection which at that time bound the Dutch Church in this country to the jurisdiction of the ecclesiastical courts in Holland, and of an independent organization, by which the training, ordination and installation of ministers, and other church business could be transacted here, by our own ecclesiastical courts. In the discussion of this question, which agitated the whole Church deeply, and which was debated with earnestness if not with acrimony for several years, he took a prominent part. The separation was finally made in 1772.*

Dr. Westerlo was also a warm patriot. During the Revolution, he took strong ground on the side of independence, and at that critical period just prior to the surrender of Burgoyne, he held special religious services in the Church daily for a week, imploring the interposition of God in behalf of our army, and animating and encouraging the people by his prayers and exhortations. He was assisted in these services by his distinguished friend, Dr. John H. Livingston, who was also his brother-in-law,† and who spent much time in Albany and its vicinity during the progress of the war.

Up to this time all the religious services in the Church were in the Dutch language. The importance of introducing the English, was however more and more felt, and in 1780, Dr. Livingston was called as colleague to preach in that language, but declined the invitation. In 1782, Dr. Westerlo began to preach half the day in English.

* See Appendix, Note F.

† They married sisters.

In this year General Washington visited Albany and had a public reception. An address on that occasion was delivered by Dr. Westerlo as the minister of the Church, and president of the consistory. The last sermon which Dr. Westerlo preached was from the 65th Psalm, 4th verse: "Blessed is the man, whom thou choosest, and causest to approach unto thee, that he may dwell in thy courts: we shall be satisfied with the goodness of thy house, even of thy holy temple."

He died on the 26th December, 1790, in the 53d year of his age. The event was somewhat sudden, though his health for some time had not been good. It excited the deepest feeling throughout the congregation. A letter written by Dr. Livingston to Dr. Meyer soon after, says: "His disease at first affected his mind, and rendered him very melancholy, but it pleased the Lord to remove all his fears and distresses; his mind became serene, and he was cheerful, established, and rejoicing in the Lord till his last moments. His house was filled with his people, who came from all parts of the city to see him, and he left them with his blessing in such a solemn manner, that it is thought he did as much good in his death as in his life.

Blessed are the dead, who die in the Lord! O that we may die the death of the righteous, and our last end be like his."

Dr. Westerlo left two children, a son Renssalaer, who was at one time a member of congress, and a daughter Catherine, who married the Hon. John Woodworth, who still survives her.

He was a man of solid learning, especially in the classics, of imposing presence, and gentle and dignified manners. Few ministers have maintained a higher standing in the Church, or a deeper place in the affections of the people. The late Harmanus Bleecker, in a sketch for Rev. Dr. Sprague's work, which I have been kindly permitted to see, and from which much of the foregoing account of Dr. Westerlo has been derived, says in closing the sketch: "Indeed so omnipresent was his religion, so engrossing his piety, that his habitual state of mind seemed to be one continued prayer, and his life an unbroken offering of praise."

In 1787, the Rev. John Bassett was settled as colleague pastor with Dr. Westerlo. He was born in Bushwick, L. I., October 1, 1764, and educated in Columbia College, N. Y. His theological studies were pursued under Dr. Livingston, and he was ordained and installed here, November 25, 1787. In December, 1804, he retired from his pastoral charge to the Boght, and afterwards to his native place on Long Island, where he died, September 4, 1824, in the 60th year of his age. He left five children, four of whom still survive. Upon his retirement from this Church, the consistory voted to pay him an annuity of $562·50 for the term of his natural life.

Mr. Bassett was a man of extraordinary erudition. He was an excellent Hebrew scholar, and excelled in classical learning. He always had several young men in his family, and under his instruction. He was a sound and edifying preacher, though not gifted with great vividness of imagination or eloquence. He had many warm friends in the congregation, who deeply regretted his departure.

The congregation at this time, as might be supposed, had grown to be very large and powerful. The population of the city was about 5,000. The Church having been in existence for nearly 150 years, the members of the congregation could not be accommodated in the old stone building, and it was decided to build a new one. The corner stone of this edifice was laid June 12, 1797. It was solemnly dedicated to the worship of Almighty God, January 27, 1799. The dedicatory discourses, on the occasion, were preached by the two pastors; Rev. Mr. Bassett, in the morning, from the 84th Psalm, 1st and 2d verses; and the Rev. Mr. Johnson, in the afternoon, from the 4th verse of the same Psalm. At that time this street presented a very different aspect from that which it wears at present. From State street, the unpaved and grassy road was lined with the ancient Dutch dwellings, with their gable ends and weathercocks, very different from the fine modern residences, which are now the homes of some of our most respectable citizens. Conspicuous among the old buildings, was the Vander Heyden palace, which stood about where the Baptist Church now stands. It was built in 1725, and taken down in 1833, and was one of the most imposing buildings of its day. But this Church edifice was in striking contrast to the buildings which then surrounded it. It rose in its massive and commanding proportions, the finest specimen of ecclesiastical architecture then in the city, and still the largest protestant house of worship, and showing, after sixty years, how faithfully it was constructed. It will now outlast many of the more showy edifices, which are at this day rising through our country. Its interior has been twice modified; once in 1820, when this pulpit was erected, and again in 1850.

In 1796, the Rev. John Barent Johnson was called to become colleague pastor with Mr. Bassett. He was born at Brooklyn, L. I., March 3, 1769. His father's name was Barent Johnson, of Dutch descent, a farmer in prosperous circumstances. His mother was Maria Guest, daughter of Capt. John Guest, of New Brunswick, who commanded a vessel which sailed from New York to Antigua. He lost both his parents before he was nine years old, and was brought up by a cousin, who was his father's executor. In his 17th year, while attending school at Flatbush, he became acquainted with the Rev. Dr. John H. Livingston, who was spending the summer there. Dr. L. discovering that he was a youth of much more than ordinary talents, encouraged him to commence a course of liberal studies, and kindly offered to receive him into his own family, and superintend his education. This offer was gratefully accepted, and he was soon prepared to enter college. In 1788 he entered Columbia College, and in the same year became a communicant in the Reformed Dutch Church. After his graduation he studied theology with Dr. Livingston; was licensed by the classis of New York, April 21, 1795, and preached his first sermon on the succeeding sabbath in that city for the Rev. Dr. Kuypers.

On the 5th of June, 1796, Mr. Johnson was ordained to the work of the ministry, and settled as colleague pastor with Mr. Bassett over this Church. His ordination sermon was preached by Mr. Bassett.

In 1802, Mr. Johnson was called to the Reformed Dutch Church in Schenectady, and also to that in Brooklyn. He decided to remove to the latter place. He preached his farewell sermon to this Church, on the 26th of September, 1802, and was installed in Brooklyn, on the 24th of the following October. Among other marked features of this sermon, which was a very able, earnest and eloquent discourse, is a fine tribute to the Heidelberg catechism, and a plea for its faithful and regular exposition in our churches. His health, which was much impaired before his removal from Albany, now began to fail rapidly, and the death of his wife, which occured in March, 1803, contributed to hasten his own. He died at the house of his brother-in-law, Peter Rosevelt, Esq., in Newtown, August 29, 1803. He left three children, two of whom still survive, in the ministry of the Episcopal Church; one at Jamaica, L. I., and another a professor in the Episcopal Theological Seminary in New York.

From a sketch of Mr. Johnson, from the pen of Hon. Teunis Van Vechten, for Rev. Dr. Sprague's work on the American Pulpit, we learn, that he was a man of unusually prepossessing personal appearance, and easy and graceful manners. "His countenance had an expression of great benignity, united with high intelligence. His manners were bland and courteous, and predisposed every one who saw him to be his friend; and his countenance and manners were a faithful index to his disposition. He was acknowledged, on all hands, to possess an uncommonly amiable and generous spirit. He had the reputation of an excellent pastor. He mingled freely and to great acceptance with all classes of people. He was particularly attentive to the young, and had the faculty of making himself exceedingly pleasant to them; this I know from personal experience.

As a preacher he was undoubtedly one of the most popular in the Dutch Church at that day. Of his manner in the pulpit, I retain a very distinct recollection. His voice was a melodious one, and though not of remarkable compass, yet loud enough to be heard with ease in a large church. His gesture was natural and effective, and sometimes he reached, what I should think, a high pitch of pulpit oratory."

At the death of General Washington the legislature of the state, then in session, requested of the consistory the use of this Church for the celebration of appropriate funeral services, and invited Mr. Johnson to deliver the eulogy on that occasion. The service was accordingly held Feb. 22d, 1800, and as might be supposed, was one of unusual interest and solemnity. The Church was hung with black, and crowded by a mourning people. The oration by Mr. Johnson was a masterly effort, and produced a great sensation. It was published by vote of both houses, Hon. Stephen Van Renssalaer, being then president of the senate, and Hon. Dirck Ten Broeck, speaker of the house. Mr. Van Vechten says of it: "The exordium was spoken of at the time, as a rare specimen of eloquence, and the whole performance was of a very high order. I speak with confidence concerning this, as it was published, and I have had the opportunity of reading it, since I have been more competent to judge of its merits than I was when it was delivered."

Mr. Van Vechten closes his sketch of Mr. Johnson in these words: "He left an excellent name behind him, and the few who still remember him, cherish gratefully the recollection of both his gifts, and his graces."

After the removal of Mr. Johnson, the Church made two unsuccessful attempts to secure a successor in the pastoral office. In Sept., 1802, a call was sent to the Rev. Henry Kollock, of Elizabethtown, and in Dec., 1802, to the Rev. Philip Milledoler, of Philadelphia, both of which were declined. In 1803, Rev. William Linn, was engaged as temporary supply, and continued to serve the Church for several years.

At the removal of Mr. Bassett in 1804, the Church was left entirely without a pastor. In the meantime it had grown to be one of the largest and most influential congregations in the state. In Feb., 1805, a call was sent to Rev. Edward D. Griffin to become the pastor, which was declined. A meeting of the Great Consistory was called afterwards, to deliberate upon its interests and to consider the subject of calling a pastor. They met on the 27th of May, 1805. Forty-nine members were present. The names of all of them are on record, and it is worthy of remark that of these forty-nine names, there are only six names which may not now be found in the congregation, although only one of the individuals who composed the meeting yet survives.* At this meeting it was decided to call the Rev. John Melancthon Bradford to the pastorate of the Church. He was required to preach but once on each sabbath during the first year of his settlement, and in case of his marriage was to receive an addition to his salary.

Mr. Bradford was born in Danbury, Conn., May 15, 1781. He was the son of the Rev. Ebenezer Bradford, then pastor of the Congregational Church in Danbury. His collegiate education was received at Brown University, R. I., where he graduated with honor. He then pursued his theological studies with the Rev. Dr. Green of Philadelphia, one of the most distinguished ministers of the Presbyterian

* The venerable Jacob Ten Eyck, Esq., of Whitehall.

Church, who was his maternal uncle. He was called to the pastoral charge of the Church in May, 1805, and having accepted the call was ordained to the office of the ministry, and installed pastor of the Church. The ordination sermon was preached by the Rev. Dr. Linn of New York.

Dr. Bradford continued in the pastoral charge about fifteen years. He was a man of fine appearance, and dignified manners, and an eloquent and impressive preacher. Few men have been better fitted by natural endowments for the position of a public speaker. His voice was uncommonly melodious, and his gesticulation dignified and graceful. His style was rich and yet chaste, and his sermons were compositions of a high order. For years he commanded large audiences, and was ranked among the distinguished pulpit orators of the day.

He died in 1827, leaving a widow and several children who yet survive. One of these, Alexander W. Bradford, now holds the office of surrogate of New York, and is a gentleman of high standing in his profession.

As early as 1799, the project of building another new church, began to receive some attention, but it was not finally decided upon till 1805. In that year the site of the old stone Church in State street was sold to the corporation of the city for $5,000, and in the spring of 1806, the venerable building, which had been occupied by the congregation for nearly a century, was taken down. For one hundred and fifty years that spot had been occupied as the site of a place of worship, and there were many sacred and touching associations connected with it. It was not strange that many hearts should feel emotions of sadness when at last it was given up to the crowd and bustle of business. The corner stone of the noble edifice now occupied by the Second Reformed Dutch Church, on Beaver street, was laid April 30th, 1806, by Rev. Dr. Bradford, and the building after several delays in the prosecution of the work was finally completed in 1810. It is one of the finest specimens of ecclesiastical architecture in this city. Indeed there are few superior to it, in our country.

In 1813, the Rev. John De Witt was called as colleague pastor with Dr. Bradford. He was a native of Catskill, the son of a farmer, who desired him to enter the profession of law. With this object he spent several years in

MIDDLE DUTCH CHURCH.

study, and graduated at Nassau Hall, in Princeton, in 1809. He then commenced the study of law in Kinderhook, but his mind having at this time been brought under deep religious impressions, he felt that it was his duty to devote himself to the work of the Christian ministry. He accordingly commenced the study of theology with the Rev. Dr. Porter of Catskill, and was first settled in the ministry in Lanesboro, Mass., in 1811. From thence he was called to become collegiate pastor with Dr. Bradford. In 1815, it was deemed advisable that the collegiate form of the Church should be abandoned, and that two distinct and independent congregations should be formed each with its own church edifice, pastor and consistory. This was carried into effect in an amicable spirit. An equitable division was made of the Church property, the two pastors drew lots for the church edifices, and the congregations connected themselves with one or the other, according to their individual choice, or convictions of duty. Dr. De Witt became the pastor of the Second or South Church. Dr. Bradford remained with the old Church, which was thereafter popularly known as the North Dutch Church.

Dr. De Witt remained pastor of the South or Second Church till September, 1823, when he was elected to the professorship of Biblical criticism, ecclesiastical history, and pastoral theology in the Theological Seminary of the Reformed Protestant Dutch Church, at New Brunswick. In this honorable and useful position he remained till his death, which occurred on the 11th of October, 1831, in the 42d year of his age.

Dr. De Witt was a man of frank, joyous, and generous nature, yet of accute and tender sensibilities. His piety was deep and ardent, and his preaching eminently plain, evangelical and earnest. His manner in the pulpit was unaffectedly dignified and serious, his voice clear and strong, and his enunciation distinct and deliberate. No man could listen to him without pleasure and instruction. As a pastor he enjoyed in a high degree the confidence and affection of his people, and his separation from them was an event deeply regretted by them all.

In October, 1824, Rev. Isaac Ferris was installed as pastor of the Second Church, and continued in that office, greatly esteemed and beloved by his people until the year 1836, when he was transferred to the pastoral charge of the Reformed Dutch Church, in Market street, New York, where he remained twelve years. He was then elected chancellor of the University of New York, in which honorable and useful position he now remains.

In Nov., 1836, the Rev. Isaac N. Wyckoff was installed pastor of the Second Church, where he still remains, after a pastorate of twenty-one years, enjoying the confidence and affection of his people. "*Serus redeat in cœlum.*"

During the ministry of Dr. Ferris, and mainly through his instrumentality, the Third Reformed Dutch Church, in this city, was organized, December 19, 1834. The first pastor was the Rev. Edwin Holmes. He was settled in February, 1835, and resigned his charge in 1840. The Rev. Andrew Yates, D. D., supplied the pulpit, and labored very efficiently and successfully in behalf of the Church, till November, 1841.

In Nov., 1841, Rev. W. H. Campbell, D. D., was installed pastor, and continued his acceptable labors till September, 1848, when he entered upon his duties, as the principal of the Albany Academy, from which he was transferred to the Theological Seminary at New

Brunswick, where he now labors with distinguished ability in the service of the church at large.

Rev. Rutgers Van Brunt was ordained and installed pastor after the removal of Dr. Campbell, but was soon obliged, by the failure of his health, to resign his charge. He was succeeded by Rev. W. W. Holloway, who remained until 1853, and then entered upon another field of labor.

The present pastor, Rev. Alexander Dickson, was installed in October, 1853, and still continues, the able and devoted minister of an affectionate people.

The retirement of Dr. Bradford, from the charge of this Church, left them again without a pastor. The pulpit was supplied for about three years by different ministers, among whom were Revds. Gabriel Ludlow, Eli Baldwin, John Kennedy, —— Bruen, R. McLeod and M. W. Dwight.

On the 31st day of August, 1822, a call was given to the Rev. John Ludlow, then professor of Biblical literature and ecclesiastical history at New Brunswick, which was accepted; and in July, 1823, Dr. Ludlow entered upon his duties as pastor of this Church. His installa-

SOUTH DUTCH CHURCH.

tion sermon was preached by the Rev. Dr. Yates, and was published at the request of the consistory.

Dr. Ludlow was born at Acquackanonck, N. J., Dec. 13, 1793. He graduated at Union College in 1814. He studied theology at New Brunswick; was licensed to preach in 1817, and in the year following was installed pastor of the First Reformed Dutch Church in New Brunswick. In June, 1819, he was elected as a professor in the Theological Seminary, from whence, in 1823, he removed to Albany. In 1834 he became provost of the University of Pennsylvania, at Philadelphia, where he remained till 1852, when he was again elected professor of ecclesiastical history, church government, and pastoral theology, at New Brunswick, which professorship he filled with distinguished ability till his death, which occurred on the 8th of September, 1857.

Of the character of Dr. Ludlow, as a man, and a minister, it is not needful that I should enlarge. His memory is too fresh and fragrant among this congregation to require that I should add anything to your own stores of knowledge. You have lately listened to an able and faithful delineation of his character, from our friend and brother, Rev. Dr. Wyckoff, and you have his discourse in your possession, as a memorial of your former pastor. Suffice it to say, that Dr. Ludlow was a bright and consistent illustration of all that distinguishes the minister of Christ. He was bold, fearless, earnest as a preacher, uncompromising in his devotion to the truth, and faithful to declare the whole counsel of God. To the hardened sinner he was a "*son of thunder*;" to the weeping penitent, a "*son of consolation.*" His ministry was much blessed of God, and there are many now who look back to him, as the earthly instrument of their conversion. The turf is yet green upon his grave, but when the storm winds of years shall have blown over it, his memory will be green and fresh in the midst of this people.

In 1828 the consistory voted to erect a parsonage, on the rear of the Church lot, and appointed a building committee for that purpose. They subsequently, and very wisely, modified that purpose, and erected the present new Consistory Room on that site, and altered the former Consistory Building into a Parsonage, which, after several additions and improvements, suggested by the liberality of the people, now furnishes a spacious and delightful residence to the pastor of the Church.

In March, 1835, the Rev. Thomas E. Vermilye, then pastor of the Congregational Church, of West Springfield, Mass., where he succeeded the Rev. Dr. Sprague, who has been for twenty-eight years the esteemed pastor of the Second Presbyterian Church in this city, was called to the pastoral care of the Church, He remained here between four and five years, enjoying a happy and prosperous ministry, and was then transferred to the Collegiate Dutch Church of New York, where for eighteen years he has labored, and where he still remains, a faithful and acceptable minister, in connection with the three excellent brethren who share with him the labors and responsibilities of that important charge.

After the removal of Dr. Vermilye, the pulpit was supplied for more than a year by Rev. John Austin Yates, D. D., then professor in Union College. Dr. Yates was a preacher of uncommon eloquence and power. His sermons made a deep impression upon the congregation, and a call was informally tendered to him, to the pastoral office, which, however, he declined.

The Rev. Duncan Kennedy, then pastor of

the Presbyterian Church in Galway, Saratoga county, was chosen to succeed Dr. Vermilye, and was installed pastor, December 22, 1841. After laboring in this field with zeal and fidelity for more than thirteen years, during some of which, large accessions were made to the Church, Dr. Kennedy, in 1855, accepted a call to the Second Presbyterian Church in Troy, where he still remains, the acceptable pastor of a large and important congregation.

In August, 1856, a call was presented to the Rev. Ebenezer P. Rogers, D. D., then pastor of the Seventh Presbyterian Church in Philadelphia, which was accepted, and he was installed pastor of this Church, November 19, 1856.

I have thus brought down the record of the history of this Church to the present time. Two hundred and fifteen years at least, have passed away, since the first minister began his labors here. What changes have been wrought in those years? Where the insignificant trading post of Fort Orange then stood, with its few hundred inhabitants, rise the domes and spires of this goodly city, with its 70,000 inhabitants, its fifty churches, its numerous commercial, manufacturing, benevolent, philanthropic and scientific institutions, the capital of a great state. The little cluster of worshipers, who sat under the instructions of Domine Megapolensis, has grown into three flourishing congregations, embracing 600 families, nearly 1,200 communicants, and nearly 2,500 souls connected with the congregations.* These three congregations are here to-day, united in the delightful duty of thanksgiving to God for all his mercies. Though three, we are one; one in our name, our origin, our faith, our polity, our spirit, and our aim. We rejoice in each other's joy; we sympathize in each other's sorrow. United as we are by so many associations and memories of the past, let us be still more closely united in the history of the future. To you, beloved brethren of our sister churches, we tender our warmest assurances of Christian love and sympathy. Your beloved pastors are heartily welcome to this pulpit. You shall always have a place in these pews; and in token of these, the sincere feelings of our hearts, for myself, and for this Church, I

*In 1857, the North Church reported to General Synod, 200 families ; communicants 407. The Middle Church, 254 families ; communicants 560. The South Church, 85 families; communicants 350.

tender to you, through your pastors, the hand of Christian fellowship.

Connected with this Church are about 200 families, embracing 1,000 souls, while our list of communicants embraces more than 400, fifty-one of whom have been added during the past year.

Have we not something then for which to render thanks to Almighty God, on this day of public thanksgiving and praise? We thank God, for our origin, our name and our history. We thank Him for that constant care and kindness which He has displayed towards us as a Church for two hundred and fifteen years. We thank Him, for the long line of able, faithful and eloquent ministers, who have gone in and out before this people in the years that are past. We thank Him for the men of piety and wisdom who have been entrusted with the government of the Church, and who having ruled well are accounted "worthy of double honor." We thank Him for the names which stand conspicuous in the history of our country, in the ranks of her soldiers, her jurists, her statesmen, her scholars, and which may be found recorded among the members of this congregation.* We thank Him for the godly men and women who have gone from the fellowship of the Church below, to that of the Church above, leaving behind them that "memory of the just," which is "blessed."

We thank Him for the memory of that devoted Foreign Missionary who went forth from the bosom of this Church to labor, and to die in the service of our Master, on heathen ground. We thank Him, that now, after two centuries have passed away, we are permitted to occupy such a distinguished place, in our denomination, and country. We thank Him for the piety, intelligence, and means of extended usefulness, which characterize us as a people to day. The old North Dutch Church while she is the senior of all other Churches in this city, is surely in a green old age, and will yield to none of her sister churches in the power of usefulness which God still gives her. Let our united thanksgivings ascend to God for all His goodness to our fathers, and to us their children. And let us feel the solemn responsibilities which our history and position devolve upon us. For to whomsoever much is given, of such shall much be required. I confess,

* See Appendix, Note G.

my friends, that the thought of this responsibility makes me tremble. And yet I am cheered and encouraged, by the many hopeful indications which the history of the past year has recorded. I would fain anticipate for this ancient Church, a glorious future. I would anticipate her progress in piety, zeal, liberality, and efficiency in her Master's service. I would rejoice in the hope that the God who was with your fathers, will be with you and your children. And when all of us have been called to leave our places, and our duties here, I rejoice to hope, and believe, that this Church will still remain, through generations yet to come, a monument of God's faithfulness to His covenant with His people, and a source of spiritual light and blessedness to this city, this country, and the world!

APPENDIX.

NOTE A.

Wessel Gansevoort and Rudolph Agricola.

These men were among the "morning stars," of the Reformation in Holland, as Wyckliffe was in England, and Huss and Jerome, in Bohemia. "They were natives of Groningen, and eminent scholars, who in the latter part of the 15th century, fifty years before Luther studied the scriptures, came to the knowledge of the doctrine of the justification by faith as well as the other cardinal doctrines of the gospel."

Through the kindness of Gen. Peter Gansevoort of this city, I have been favored with the following account of Wessel Gansevoort, which was obtained by Hon. Harmanus Bleecker, during his residence at the Hague, from authentic documents in Holland.

Jan Wessel Hermansz. (son of Herman) Gansfort or Ganzefoort, was born at Groningen in the year 1419. After the loss of his parents he was brought up by a respectable lady of that place, to whom his mother was related. She sent him with her son of the same age, to Zwolle, that he might there, in the flourishing school of the Brotherhouse, acquire the rudiments of learning. He afterwards pursued his studies at Cologne;

where from the Greek, the study of which was not permitted in his own country, he acquired a more thorough knowledge of the original text of the New Testament.

Subsequently he resided for some time at Heidelberg and Louvain; also long at Paris and in Rome; in all which places he endeavored to be useful, by instructing in several sciences, especially in philosophy, in which he followed the opinion of Plato. But what he taught with most fondness was the Christian theology. In this he was frequently opposed by the priests, who admired, but hated him. Whenever he found no hindrance, he shed on this subject, an unusual light, which was received by the intelligent, and handed down to posterity. Finally, when he was fifty years old, he established himself in his native city, Groningen. Here he spent the remnant of his days in the Cloister of the Holy Virgins, and died on the 4th of October 1489. In the meanwhile, he passed much time in the Abbey of ——— not far from Groningen, where there was then a very celebrated school, over which he acquired an unlimited influence. As he was an uncommonly learned man, he also exceeded all his cotemporaries in the knowledge of theology. He taught that the holy scriptures were the only rule of faith and godliness, rejecting as such a rule, the traditions of the church, the decrees of councils, and the writings of the fathers. He taught that the righteousness of Christ was imputed to us by faith, and that no one could be saved by the righteousness of the law; that the holy sacrament was desecrated by the abuse of the mass; that by indulgencies a commerce was carried on utterly opposed to the doctrine of the Gospel concerning the forgiveness of sins; that the notion of a purgatory as it was maintained by the priesthood, must be viewed as a chimera; that in so far as the pope has a supremacy, he is by no means infallible;

that he can not forgive sins, &c. In consequence of all this, Luther long afterwards perceived that Gansevoort had thought exactly like him; and made this just observation, that it would appear to the enemies of the Reformation that he had read the writings of this man, and borrowed from them all his opinions. But notwithstanding this was not entirely the case, it was matter of great joy to him that he had been so confirmed in his opinions. Erasmus had before made the same observation in relation to Luther, compared with Gansevoort, adding however that the last had brought forward everything with a more moral and Christian property than the former, and the greater part of his followers. Luther also acknowledged this, and ascribed it to this alone, that Gansevoort had not been able to advance the work of the Reformation beyond the circle of his friends at, and in the neighborhood of Groningen, and thus had been only a forerunner of the Reformation.

All the writings of Gansevoort, have been collectively published at several places and times. The first edition at Wittemberg in the year 1521, under the superintendence of, and with a preface by Luther. Other editions followed long afterwards at Arnhem, and at Groningen, in the year 1614, and at Marburg in the year 1617.

Agricola, on the other hand, was distinguished for his attainments in Greek and Latin literature, and in various sciences. He spent a great part of his life as a professor at Heidelberg, and preceded Erasmus in applying a knowledge of Greek to the critical examination of the New Testament. In theological views, he harmonized with his friend and countryman Gansevoort. The seed sown by these men was quickened into life by the Reformation.—(*Demarest's History and Characteristics of the Reformed Protestant Dutch Church.*)

NOTE B.

Although we have not been able to find the record of the labors of any minister before the arrival of Domine Megapolensis in 1642, yet from the allusion in his call, as well as from the character of the Hollanders, there is reason to suppose that the institutions of religion were planted in the colony at an earlier day. The Collegiate Church in New York is said by some to have been organized as early as 1619. Among the manuscripts of the late Rev. Dr. Livingston, there is reference to a list of the members of that church in 1622. But Dr. Livingston also says in another of his manuscripts that "in Albany they had ministers as early as any in New York, if not before them." It is certainly possible, that the first church organized in this country, was the church in Albany.

NOTE C.

The following additional particulars respecting Domine Megapolensis, we gather from Vol. III of the New York Historical Society Collections, from the pen of J. Romeyn Brodhead, Esq.

"Nor were the pious services of Megapolensis confined to his own countrymen. A part of his duty was to "edify and improve" the savages in the neighborhood. He therefore applied himself diligently to the task of learning what he termed the "heavy language" of the Mohawks, so as to be able to speak and preach to them fluently. The Red men around Fort Orange or Beverwyck were soon attracted to hear the preaching of the gospel; Megapolensis, the first protestant Dutch clergyman on the northern frontier of New Netherland, thus gave, in 1643, the example of missionary zeal, which, three years afterwards, in 1646, was imitated, near Boston, by John Eliot, the "Morning Star" of a similar enterprise in New England.

"An incident occurred about this time, which should not be omitted in any notice of Domine Megapolensis. Father Isaac Jogues, a noble-hearted and self-denying Jesuit missionary, while on his way from Quebec to the Chippeways, was taken prisoner by the Mohawks, and suffered horrible cruelties from the savages. During the winter of 1642–3, however, some of his persecutors began to listen to his teachings, and his situation was so far improved that he was allowed to make occasional visits, with parties of the Mohawks, to the neighboring Dutch at Fort Orange, who did all they could to effect his deliverance. At length Jogues eluded the vigilance of the savages, and remained for several weeks in close concealment, during which constant kindness was shown him by Domine Megapolensis, who had become his warm friend. The Jesuit father was eventually ransomed by the Dutch, and sent down to Manhattan, whence he sailed for Europe. Jogues returned to Canada in 1646, and again visited the Mohawks, by whom he was cruelly put to death.

"In 1644, two years after his settlement at Beverwyck, Domine Megapolensis drew up the tract entitled *Korte Ontwerp van de Mahakuase Indianen in Nieuw Nederlandt*, &c., or, "A Short Sketch of the Mohawk Indians in New Netherland, &c." This little work is said by Van der Donck (N. Y. H. S. Coll. [II. Series], i, p. 158,) to have been in the form of a letter written to his friends in Holland, by whom it appears to have been published—as the domine himself said—"without his consent." Van der Donck, who is very competent authority, adds, that it "may be fully credited, he [Megapolensis] being a man of truth and of great learning, who writes in a vigorous style." The domine's tract gives a very interesting account of the Mohawk Indians, their habits and customs, of which but little was then known in Holland. * * * * *

"Megapolensis never lost his interest in the Mohawk savages, among whom he had spent his early years in the province. His letters to the classis of Amsterdam contain several interesting details concerning them, from whom he obtained the missal and other memorials of his murdered friend, the missionary Father Jogues. In 1658, another Canadian Jesuit, Simon Le Moyne, who, in the summer of 1654, had discovered the salt springs at Onondaga, visited New Amsterdam, and became quite intimate with Megapolensis. He related to him his discovery at Onondaga, which the domine communicated to the classis in Holland, adding, however, a somewhat uncourteous expression of his doubt of the fact. Le Moyne seems to have been very anxious to effect the conversion of his Dutch clerical friend to the Romish doctrine, and wrote three polemical essays, which he sent to Megapolensis, after his return to the North. The domine, however, not shaken in his faith, prepared a reply to the father, which he dispatched to him by a bark which sailed from New Amsterdam for Quebec. But the vessel—which was the first that cleared from Manhattan for Canada—on entering the Saint Lawrence was wrecked on the Island of Anticosti, and Le Moyne lost the benefit of the domine's elaborate answer. * * * * * * *

"Megapolensis, after seven years' service at Beverwyck, and twenty years' labor at Manhattan, died in the discharge of his pastoral functions. He was a man of thorough scholarship, energetic character, and devoted piety; and he is entitled to high, if not preeminent position, in the roll of early protestant missionaries among the North American savages. For nearly a quarter of a century he exercised a marked influence in the affairs of New Netherland. He saw the infancy of the Dutch province, watched its growth, and witnessed its surrender to overpowering English force. His name must ever be associated with the early history of New York, towards the illustration of which his correspondence with the classis of Amsterdam, now in the possession of the general synod of the Reformed Protestant Dutch Church, and this sketch of the Mohawk Indians, form original and very valuable contributions."

The Baptismal Register

For 1690 contains the following names of Indian converts:

	Age.	Bap. Name.
Sucongara (Little Plank),...........	40,	David,
Kowajatense (his wife),............	30,	Rebecca,
Tekaneadaroga,..................	22,	Isaac,
Tejonihokarawe (Open the Door),...	30,	Hendrick,
Karanondo (Uplifter),.............	50,	Lydia,
Kaadejiheudara,..................	12,	Seth,
Siouheja (Lively),................	..	Rachel,
Skanjodowanne (Eagle's Beak),.....	..	Manasse,
Sagonorasse (Fast Binder),.........	12,	Adam,
Karehodongwas (The Plucker),.....	16,	Eunice,
———— (Son of Eunice),....	9 mos.	Simon,
Kwaorate (Mother of Eunice),......	60,	Leah,
Karehojenda (Daughter of Leah),...	30,	Alida,
Waniho,.........................	40,	Josine,
Daughter of Josine, ...	9,	Jakomina,
Son of Josine,....................	7,	Joshua.

NOTE D.

Petition for Rebuilding the Dutch Church in Albany.

To His Excellency Robert Hunter Esqr Cap[t] Generall and Governour in Chief of the provinces of New York New Jersey and Territories thereon Depending in America and vice Admirall of the Same &c

The Humble Petition of Petrus van Driesen Minister of the Nether Dutch Reformed Congregation of the City and County of Albany and the Elders and Deacons of the said Congregation, Humbly Sheweth

That the Predecessors of your Excellency's humble Petitioners in the year of our Lord 1655 & 1656 when this towne was Settled did with assistance of the then nether dutch Congregation build and Erect at their own proper Cost and Charge the Church belonging to the said congregation (Standing & being in the said City) for their Christian devotion and Publick worship of Almighty god, in the Exercise of the Reformed protestant Religion, which Church is Since been Confirmed to the Mayor Alderman & Commonalty of y[e] Said City by Charter, under the Seale of the Province.

That the said Church being built of timber & boards is by time so much decayd that they find themselves under the necessity of building a new one in its place and your Petitioners believing your Excellencys Continance and approbation will be very advantageous to them, in this their undertaking.

Your Excys Petitioners do therefore most humbly pray that your Excellency will please to approve and Encourage this pious work by signifying such your approbation and your petitioners as in duty bound shall Ever pray &c

PETRUS VAN DRIESSEN V. D. Præco
JOHANNES ROOSEBOOM
MYNDERT SCHUYLER
HENDR VAN RENSSELAER
JOHANNES BEEKMAN
RUTGERT BLEECKER
STEVANIE GROESBECK

I do approbe of what is desired In the petition and recommend the Same to all who are concernd

18 June 1714 RO: HUNTER

INTRODUCTION TO MR. VAN DRIESSEN'S THREE DISCOURSES.

We give below the introduction to three sermons by Rev. Mr. Van Driessen, two of which were preached on the accession of King George I to the throne of Great Britain, and one on the occasion of Gov. Burnet's treaty with the Five Nations. The sermons were printed in 1726:

To his Excellency *WILLIAM BURNET*, Esq; Captain General and Governour in Chief of the Provinces of *New-York*, *New-Jersey*, and the Territories depending thereon in *America*, and Vice Admiral of the same, &c.

May it please Your Excellency:

Of Ancient Times certain Princes of this World, thro' the Greatness of their Souls, have made themselves renowned; so that several Princes are famed, that They held the Scepter in their left Hand, but the Pen in their Right: And thence the old Proverb, *HIS PRÆVIDE ET PROVIDE*; that they might not only show themselves ready and capable for the Execution of those Affairs, confided and subjected to them, but were also willing to prove the Elevation of their Souls (called by *Aristotle* the Lord of Nature) by applying and explaining themselves in their Studies of noble Sciences: *Cassidorus* calls it *the Crown and Lustre of the Majesty of Princes,* as of a far greater Lustre in a Crown than precious Stones, and more Excellent than the best of Jewels.

This Nobleness of Mind has not a little contributed to the good Management of their Affairs; thereby evincing that they were capable to Execute such Matters as were fitting for their Grandeur.

In the Picture of *Cæsar,* standing upon a Globe, he is seen holding a Sword in one Hand and a Pair of Scales in the other, with this Motto, *ON BOTH SIDES CÆSAR;* whereby we are taught, that in Government an illuminated Judgment, as well as the Use of Arms, was necessary: Therefore it was very pertinently said by the Ancients, *Good Learning is Silver in the common People, Gold in the Nobles, but in the Princes precious Stones:* Yea, the Holy Scriptures exalts them yet above all those Excellencies; so Wisdom in such Persons is glorifying her Government, as they are thereby glorified.

I having the Honour and Happiness to know Your Excellency, not only in your Chief Government of these *American* Provinces, but also as being endued with the noble Attributes of a zealous Lover of noble Sciences and Languages; thereby continually animating Your great Soul to a further Progress in sound Knowledge, both of Divine and Temporal Matters, to the greater Lustre of Your Excellency and Advancement in Reputation and Grandeur.

So that the Greatness of Soul of your deceased Father revives in you, who exceeded in all what may be called Learning, many of his Cotemporaries, and as such was highly esteemed and loved by Foreigners, as also for his Zeal for the true Religion, manifested as the Flower and Lustre of Pious Men, when the Mystery of Iniquity was in Travel and brought forth Vanity, at the Time when his Honour published his History of the Reformation; and shewed himself moreover, with many others, a vigilant Defender of that blessed Constitution in Church and State, whereof we now enjoy the pleasant Fruits, which will cause him to be admired by our Posterity in many Ages, and therefore to live forever in the Remembrance of us and ours.

How just is then the Oppinion of such who are assured hereof, and have the Honour to know Your Excellency, and have spied out Your innate Love to Learning, and that Your Excellency may be numbered among those that are said to *Patrizare*, I mean to succeed their renowned Parents in their excellent Virtues. *Aristotle* said once, ***It** is likely that those are better that draw their Pedigree from the Good.* To that End we read in *Horace*,

Fortes creantur Fortibus, & Bonis.
Est in Juvencis, est in Equis Partum
Virtus: nec imbellem feroces
Progenerunt Aquillæ Collumbam.

Your Excellency honoured me with your Presence when I treated of *The Apointment of the Powers of this World, by the Divine Jesus; on the occasion of Your Excellency's treating with the Five Nations of Indians,* upon *Prov.* VIII, 14,-16. Doing me the Honour to desire that Sermon of me; far from it that I should have formed the least Thoughts that would have been unwilling to shew my Readiness to satisfy Your Excellency, that, on the contrary, I not only concluded to dedicate the same to your Excellency, but also to joyn thereunto *Solomons Coronation and Exaltation to the Throne, on Occasion of his Majesty King* George's *Accession to the Crown and Throne of* Great Britain; upon 1 *Reg.* I, 36,-40. A Matter brought forth from the sincere Inclination of my Heart, which I have to our present Sovereign Lord *GEORGE*, by the Grace of GOD, King of *Great Britain*, and my Desire for the Establishing the *Protestant* Being. A happy Establishment, which we are to look upon as a happy Consequence and Effect of the Actions of the great and prevoyant King *William* the third, of glorious Memory, and his faithful Ministers of State, who certainly effected it *plura Concilio quam Vi.* An Establishment, nevertheless, which we ought peculiarly to ascribe to the Providence of the most High. So that we must acknowledge, that this great Event depends more on the divine Council than on the Power or Wisdom of Men.

Hereunto I have added, *The Scaffold of Felonious Traitors against their lawful Sovereign Lord* George, *King of* Great Britain, *erected and exposed to View;* upon *Psal.* LXII, 3,-7. In Expectation that this Sermon would be no less pleasant to Your Excellency than the former, considering Your Love for the Kings Happiness and Zeal for the Commonwealth. They who designed to dethrone their lawful Sovereign King *GEORGE*, are deceived in their Enterprize, and all their Designs are fallen out to their Shame. A Prove of the horrid Perversness of *Antichristian Malignants*, wickedly designing to change the Protestant Religion into *Papal Tyranny.*

For the rest, with this Dedication I do express my Acknowledgment and Esteem for Your Excellency's penetrating Judgment in noble Sciences; as also my Duty to You, as my Superiour Governour; my Desire is that they may serve as a Token of my Gratitude for the especial Favours wherewith Your Excellency has honoured me during my Abode here.

And my Prayer to the Alsufficient God is, *That he endue Your Excellency with more Wisdom, and make You more and more capable to execute those high Powers of Government, under the Divine Providence entrusted unto You by His Majesty, and that according to the best Policy, to the Wellbeing of Church and State; and that especially the Affairs of the Kingdom, which are here of great Consequence, may, under Your good Government, be happy and flourish.*

To which End the Lord grant you Wise, Faithful and Wellmeaning Counsellors, to make Your Government the more praiseworthy, and the Inhabitants happy and prosperous.

Yea, the Lord crown Your Person, Government and Family with Grace and Honour, in Length of Days.

This Desires, Wishes and Prays,

May it please Your Excellency,

Your Excellency's faithful, and ready Servant in the Lord,

PETRUS VAN DRISSEN.

NOTE E.

EARLY MEMBERS OF THE CHURCH.

We give below the list of members from 1683, as they stand upon the records of the Church in the handwriting of Mr. Dellius:

Juriaan Teunis,
Ariaentje Teunis,
Abraham Staats,
Tryntje Staats,
Willem Teller,
Marritje Teller,
Jan Becker,
Mari Becker,
Aarnout Cornelis Vilen,
Gerrigje Vilen,
Andries Teller,
Sephia Teller,
Johannes Provoost,
Cornelis Van Dyck,
Lysbet Van Dyck,
Catryn Rutgirs,
Anaetje Lives (married Goosen Gerritsen Van Scayck, July, 1657),
Jochum Staats,
Lysbet Bancker,
Margeriet Schuyler,
Richart Pritti,
Lysbet Pritti,
Annetje Staats,
Jan Tomes,
Geertruyt Tomes,
Jacob Schermerhorn (immigrated 1645?),
Janetje Schermerhorn (da. of Cornelis Segers),
Meindert Herman (Van Den Bogert),
Heleen Hermans (his wife, and da. of Jacob Jans Schermerhorn),
Evert Wendel the Father,
Merritje Wendels,

Johannes Wendell,
Lysbet Wendell (now Schuyler),
Hendrick Cuyler,
Annetje Cuyler,
Henderick Rosenboom,
Gysbertje Rosemboom (da. of —— Lansing),
Jan Ouderkerck,
Dirck Wesselse Ten Brouck,
Styntje Ten Brouck (da. of Cornelis Maasen Van Beuren ?),
Marten Krygier,
Jannetje Krygier (da. of —— Hendricks),
Adriaan Gerrits (Papendorp),
Jannetje Gerrits (his wife),
Gerrit Swart,
Antonia Swart,
Wouter Van Den Uythost,
Leendert Phlipsen (Conyn),
Agnietje Leenderts (his wife),
Anna Van der Heyden,
Arien Van Elpendam,
Gerrit Van Esch,
Marietje Van Esch,
Hermen Tomes (Hun?),
Catelyntje Tomes (his wife)
Anna Kettel,
Grietje Gouws (she is dead)
Taakel Dircks,
Marritje Taakels (his wife),
Wynand Gerrits (Van der Poel),
Tryntje Wynands (his wife)
Pieter Loockerman,
Marretje Lookermans,
David Schuyler,
Catelyntje Schuyler,
Pieter Mees Vrooman,
Folikje Vrooman,
Jacob Mees Vrooman,
Lysbeth Vrooman,
Aalbert Ryckman,
Nelletje Ryckman,
Sybrent Van Schayck,
Lysbet Van Schayck (now Corlaar),
Jacob Staats,
Ryckje Staats,
Willem Percker,
Maria Percker,
Robbert Levinchston,
Alida Levinchston (da. of —— Schuyler),
Philip Freest,
Tryntje Freest (da. of —— Kip),
Gerrit Hardenberch,
Joapje Hardenberch,
Abraham Van Tricht,
Lysbeth Van Tricht (now Vanderpoel),
Symen (Jacobs) Schermerhorn,
Wilmje Schermerhorn (now Winnen),

Johannes de Wandelaar,
Sara de Wandelaar (da. of —— Schep-Moes).
Johannes Van Sandt,
Margeriet Van Sant,
Melchert Wynandts (Vanderpoel).
Areaantje Wynandts (his wife).
Laurens Van Alen,
Elbertje Van Alen,
Tryntje Rutten (now Roseboom),
Jan Jans Bleecker,
Grietjen Bleecker (da. of —— Van Schoendemund),
Jan Byvang,
Belia Byvang,
Gerrit Lansing,
Elsje Lansing,
Hendrick Lansing,
Lysbet Lansing,
Jan Lansing,
Geertje Lansing,
Jan Nack,
Jan Vinhagel,
Marretje Vinhagel,
Geertje Bout,
Willem Bout,
Luycas Gerrits,
Antje Lucas,
Isaac Verplanck,
Abigail Verplanck (da. of —— Bogert),
Johannes Beeckman,
Machtelt Beeckman (da. of Jacob J. Schermerhorn),
Nicolaas Van Rotterdam,
Lysbet Van Rotterdam,
Harmen Bastiaans (Visscher),
Hester Bastiaans (da. of —— Turk),
Robbert Sanders (Glen?),
Elsje Sanders (Glen),
Jacob Sanders (Glen),
Caatje Sanders (now Douw)
Nicolaas Rips,
Marie Nicolaas Rips,
Jacob Coenraats,
Geertje Jacobs (his wife),
Johannes Roosenboom,
Margeriet Roosenboom,
Jan Cloet,
Bata Cloet (da. of —— Slightenhast),
Pieter Davids Schuyler,
Alida Schuyler (da. of Slightenhast),
Guysbert Marselis,
Barbar Marselis (his wife, da. of Claas Jacobs Groesbeck),
Willem Claes Groesbeeck,
Geertruyt Groosbeeck (da. of —— Schuyler),
Johannes Roos,
Cornelia Roos,
Jan Gilbert,
Cornelia Gilbert (da. of —— Van den Bergh),
Evert Wendel (the son),
Lysbeth Wendel (da. of —— Glen),

Cornelis Scherluyn,
Geertruyt Scherluyn (da. of Harman B. Visscher),
Rachel Rettle,
Jacob Loockerman,
Tryntje Loockerman,
Caatje Lookerman (now Ten Brock),
Jacob Abrahams,
Catelyntje Jacobs (his wife)
Nicolaes Van Elslant,
Aaltje Frans (Pruyn),
Johannes Appel,
Anetje Appel,
Johannes Tomes (Mingaal),
Mari Jans (Mingall, da. of Jan Jans Oothout),
Jacobus Turck,
Caatje Turck (da. of Van Benthuisen),
Levinus Van Schayck,
Margaret Van Schayck,
Henderick Bries,
Marie Bries (now Lokermans),
Reimer Barents,
Bastiaan Harmens (Visscher),
Dirckje Bastiaans (his wife, and da. of Teunis Teunisse de Metselaar),
Maas Cornelis (Van Buren),
Jacomyn Maas (his wife),
Willem Guysberts (Van den Bergh),
Catryn Willems (his wife),
Cornelis Gysberts (Van den Bergh),
Pieter Winne,
Tanne Winne,
Levinus Winne,
Jan Salomons (Goewey),
Caatje Salomons (his wife), and da. of —— Lookerman),
Barbar Salomons (Goewey)
Dirck Bensing,
Fytje Bensing,
Lysbet Herris (now Kaer),
Huybertje Jeedts,
Pieter Schuyler,
Engeltje Schuyler,
Arent Schuyler,
Maria Van Renselaar,
Ciliaan Van Renselaar,
Anna Van Renselaar,
Teunis (Cornelis) Van der Poel,
Catryn Van der Poel,
Anna Van der Poel,
Hendrick Van Esch,
Annetje Van Esch,
Luycas Pieters (Coeyman),
Ariaantje Lucas (his wife),
Adam Winnen,
Anna Winnen (now Teunisse),
Marten Jans,
Jannetje Martens (his wife, and da. of ——Cornelis),
Marritje Quakelbosch,
Douwe Jelis (died Nov. 27, 1700),

Rebecca Douws (his wife),
Wouter Quakelbosch,
Neeltje Quakelbosch,
Jan (Pieters) Quakelbosch,
Machtelt Quakelbosch (da. of Jan Post),
Reinier (Pieters) Quakelbosch,
Lysbit Quackelbosch,
Folekje Brabanders,
Margriet Ketel,
Ysbrant Elders,
Jan de Noorman (the elder)
Marritje Noorman (now Carbith),
Jan (Andries) Douw,
Catryn Douw,
Arien Appel,
Wouter de Rademmaecker,
Grietje Wouters (his wife),
Gerrit Reyers,
Annetje Reyers,
Marretje Van Schayck,
Geertje Brickers,
Marretje Zacharias,
Robbert Sickels,
Cornelis Van der Hoeven,
Metje Van der Hoeven,
Merselis Jans,
Annetje Marselis (his wife),
Pieter Bogardus,
Wyntje Bogardus (da. of Cornelis Bosch),
Marten Gerrits (Van Bergen),
Jannetje Martens (his wife, Nieltje Myndert, 2d wife)
Teunis Cornelis (Van Vechten),
Hester Teunissen (his wife)
Geertje Van der Hoeven,
Jurian Coller,
Lysbeth Coller,
Andries de Sweed (i. e., Andries Alberts Bratt),
Neeltje Andries (da. of Teunis Sway),
Teunis Slingerlandt,
Celia Slingerlant,
Jan Hendricks (Van den Bergh),
Maria Jans,
Jan Van der Hoeven,
Jannetje Ver Wey,
Sara Ketel,
Sela Ketel (now Rachel Van der Heyden),
Antje Cross,
Paulyn Jans,
Wyntje Paulyns (his wife),
Ryck Michiels,
Jannetje Paulyns,
Anna Pieterse (Van Slyck),
Hendrick Maes (Van Beuren),
Lysbeth Hendricks (his wife),
Gerrit Gysberts (Van den Berg),
Teuntje Gerrits (his wife),
Frerick de Drent,
Jannetje Vries (now Salsberry),
Hendrick Marselis,

Barent Pieters (Coeyman),
Jacob Salomons (Goewey),
Lyntje Salomons (his wife),
Geertruyt Rinckhout,
Mattys Hooghteeling,
Maria Hooghteeling,
Jan Jacobs Van Oostrant,
Agnient Van Oostrant,
Phlip Leenderts (Conyn),
Wyntje Phlips (his wife, and da. of —— Dirks),
Gerrit Lamberts (Van Valkenburgh),
Marie Jochems,
Dirck Teunis (Van der Vechten),
Jannetje Dircks (rather Van der Vechten),
Gerrit Teunis (Van der Vechten),
Grietje Gerrits (Van der Vechten),
Magdeleen Quakelbosch,
Andries Jans (Witbeck),
Jan Bronck,
Commertje Bronck (da. of Lendert Conyn),
Melchert Abrams (Van Deusen),
Engeltje Abrams (his wife),
Hendrick Abels (Riddenhaas),
Sephia Abels (now Nak),
Johannes (Jans) Oothout,
Hendrick (Jans) Oothout,
Jacobus Jans,
Jannetje Jacobs (his wife),
Mayken Jacobus,
Abraham Van Breemen,
Marretje Van Bremen,
Johannes Jans (Witbeck),
Lysbet Jans (Witbeck, da. of Leendert Conyn),
Claes Van Petten,
Isje Van Petten,
Cornelis Teunis Van Vechten),
Annetje Cornelis (his wife),
Marten Cornelis (Van Beuren),
Marretje Martens (his wife)
Cornelia Martens (now Van Deusen),
Angeltjie Andries (wife of Andries Jans Witbeck ?),
Geertje Gysberts,
Hendrick Ver Wey,
Teunis de Metselaar,
Egbertje Teunis (his wife),
Wilmje Teunis (now Bratt)
Symen Schouten,
Cypjen Schouten,
Andries Hans,
Gerretje Andries (his wife, and da. of Teunis Teunisse de Metselaar),
Isje Hans,
Jacob Van Oostrant,
Mees Hogenboom,
Catryn Hogenboom,
Ariaantje Hogenboom,
Antoni Van Schayck,
Marietje Van Schayck (da. of —— Van der Poel),

Roeloff Gerrits,
Geertruyt Roelofs (his wife)
Jan Grutters,
Hermen Lievens,
Marretje Hermens (Lieversen),
Jan Van Esch,
Aaltje Van Esch,
Barent Bratt,
Susanna Bratt,
Geurt Hendricks,
Marretje Geurten (his wife)
Andries Carstels,
Harmen Jans Knickelbacker,
Lysbet Harmens (his wife, and da. of —— Bogert),
Wessel Ten Broeck,
Elsje Ten Broeck (now Cuyler),
Lambert Van Valkenborgh,
Alida Vinhagel (now Visscher),
Gysje Vanderheyden (now Geesje Kip),
Cornelia Van der Heyden,
Jan Tysens Hoes (i. e. Goes ?),
Styntje Hoes,
Jochum Lamberts (Van Valkenburgh),
Eva Jochum (his wife, da. of —— Vrowman),
Pieter Vosburgh,
Jannetje Pieters (Vosburgh)
Geertruyt Vosburgh,
Maria Jacobs (now Van Vechten),
Jan Martens,
Dirckje Jans (his wife),
Aalbert (Jacobs) Gerdenier,
Marretje Aalberts (his wife)
Jannetje Lamberts (Van Volkenburgh),
Tam Kreeve,
Jannetje Kreeve,
Aaltje Adams,
Teuwis Cool,
Marretje Teuwis (his wife),
Ariaantje Hendriks,
Teuwis Abrams,
Helena Teuwis (his wife),
Samson Bensing,
Tryntje Samsons (his wife, a Mathus),
Johannes Bensing,
Mattys Hooghteeling,
Nanning Harmens (Visscher),
Cornlis Stephens (Muller),
Hilletje Cornelis (a Lookerman his wife),
Caasper Leenderts (Conyn)
Colette Caspars (Winnen his wife),
Mayken Martens,
Isabella Dellius,
Dorete Volkens (Douw ?),
Catryntje Volkens (Douw?)
Maria Schuyler (now Van Dyck),
Mayken Jacobs,

Anerigje Jans,
Phlip Wendell,
Bastian Harmans (Visscher)
Rebecca Everts (wife of —— Hanssen),
Hester Bricker (now Slingerland),
Aaltje Arents,
Andries Jans,
Barentje Jans,
Jonas Volkens (Douw),
Chilian Winne,
Thomas Winne,
Barentje Vollewever (surnamed Schaats),
Jacob Teunis Van Schoonderwooert,
Margaret Van Dam,
Hester Harmens (Visscher)
Willemyntje Nack,
Sara Cuyler (now Van Brugge),
Maria Sanders (now Roseboom),
Gerritje Costers (now Roseboom),
Alida Everts (now Oothout)
Paulus Martens Van Benthuysen,
Wouter Pieters Quakelbosch,
Pieter Hendrick De Haas,
Pieter Tomes Mingaal,
Helena Byvang,
Rebecca Claes (Groesbeck ? now Van Schaak),
Catelyntje Ten Brouck,
Martina Bicker (now Hoogen),
Susanna Wendel,
Benony Van Corlar,
Jan Ratlife,
Antje Van Esch (now Ridder),
Martina Teunis,
Cornelia Ten Broeck,
Susanna Barents,
Sara Sanders (now Greevenrood),
Marie Katelyne (now Bratt)
Dyrckje Luyckens,
Antje Becker,
Abraham Staats, Jr.,
Elbert Gerrits,
Jan Huyberts,
Johannes Bleycker, Jr.,
Antoni Bries,
Gerrit Lansing, Jr.,
Herbert Jacobs (Van Deusen),
Hendrick Rosenboom, Jr.,
Jan Abeel,
Maria Parcker,
Catryn Villeroy,
Sarah Hardenberch,
Annetje Lives,
Abraham Cuyler,
Dirck Barents Bratt,
Solomon Frederick Booch,
Elizabeth Van Gelder,
Symon Van Esch,
Catharine Van Schayck,

Deborah Van Dam (wife of Hendrick Hansse),
Margriet Jurries,
Zytje Marselis (wife of Joseph Jansse),
Est de Ridder,
Cornelis Martens,
Jacob Vosbergh,
Isaac Vosberch,
Abraham Jans (Van Alstyne ?),
Lambert Jans (Van Alstyne ?),
Isaac Jans (Van Alstyne ?),
Dorotche Vosburgh,
Teuntje Jans (Van Alstyne? now Winnen),
Manetje Vosburgh,
Anna Vosburgh,
Geertruy Sickles,
Est Bancker,
Elizabeth Bancker(an Abeel his wife),
David Christiaans,
Abraham Isaacks,
Anna Sickels,
Cornelia Van Male,
Johannes Schuyler,
Margriet Schuyler,
Cornelia Vroman,
Lysbeth Lansing(now Bratt
Judick Marselis (wife of Lucas Lucasy),
Andries Hans Huyck,
Catryn Andries (a Van Valkenburgh his wife),
Cornelia Tys (Goes ?),
Geertruy Jans Witbeck (now wife of Barent Gerritsen),
Marretje Hendericks (now Schermerhorn),
Ariaantje Gerrits,
Lyntje Winne (now Witbeek),
Lysbeth Rosenboom (now Van Deusen),
Johanna Bratt (now Keteluyn),
Henderikje Van Schoonhoven (now Poppi),
Ariaantje Van Schoonhoven,
Frans Pieters Clauw,
Elsje Fransen Clauw,
Adam Dingman,
Geertje Martens,
Geertruy Ten Broeck (now Schuyler),
Anna de Peyster,
Annetje Gerrits,
Eytje Pieters,
Caatje Bleycker (now Cuyler),
Eva Vinhagel (now Beekman),
Willem Jacobs (Van Deusen),
James Willet,
Maria Wendell,
Abraham Kip,
Henderick Greefradt,

Johannes Pruyn,
Jan Jans Post,
Johannes Bratt,
Huybert Gerrits,
Rut Melcherts,
Cornelis Gerrits,
Anna Sanders,
Maria Van Renssalaer (now Schuyler),
Jacomyntje Vile,
Mayken Oothout (wife of Thomas Harmensen, Jr.?)
Coatje Melcherts (Van der Poel ? now Witbeck),
Jannetje Cobus,
Rachel Melcherts (Van der Poel ?),
Cornelia Coljer,
Catarine Van Allen (now Van der Poel),
Nelletje Quakelbosch,
Francyntje Hendericks,
Geertruy Hogenboom,
Neeltje Slingerlandt,
Engletje Lives,
Geertruy Jans,
Margriet Brickers,
Susanna Lansing,
Hermen Rutgers,
Cornelia Van Vreedenburch (now Van Yselsteyn),
Hester Davids,
Weyntje Fransen (Clauw?),
Judick (Jans) Van Housen,
Henderick Van Renssalaer,
Joseph Jans,
Jan Fondaas,
Marretje Van Petten (now Van Allen),
Catelyntje Van Petten (now Van Vechten),
Margaret Hans (now Visscher),
Henderick Van Dyck,
Abraham Schuyler,
Cornelia Van Olinda,
Arieentje Vanderheyden.

On July 11th, 1690, the following Indians:

Paulus,
Laurens,
Maria.

On October 22d, 1691, the following Indians:

David,
Rebecca,
Lydia.

At the same time the following persons:

Sarah Harmens (Visscher),
Marretje Gerrits,
Jannetje Blyker,
Marretje Vanhagel,
Anna Coster.

On March 24th, 1692, the following Indians:

Isak,
Rachel,
Rebecca,
Eunice.

At the same time the following persons:
Meindert Schuyler,
Jacobus Van Dyck,
Johannes Rykman,
Willem Van Allen,
Tammus Noxen,
Luthers Jans (Witbeck),
Andries Douw,
Pieter Lucas Koeyman,
Debora Staats (now Roseboom),
Elsje Rutgers (now Schuyler),
Maria Banker,
Anna Gansevoort,
Christina Ten Broek,
Antje Van der Heyden,
Marietje Pruyn (wife of Elbert Gerretsen,
Rachel Cuyler (now Schuyler),
Tryntje Rykman (now Breese),
Marritje Lookerman (now Fonda),
Marritje Bogardus (now Van Vechten),
Grietje Takel,
Barbar Jans (wife of Gerrit Rikse),
Elsje Wendell (now Staats),
Jannetje Oothout (Van Schaack).

September 17th, 1692.

Canastasji (Indian),
Gerrit Rosenboom,
Pieter Verbrugge,
Stephanus Groesbeeck.

December 23d, 1692.

Henderik (Indian).

April 13th, 1693.

Antoni Coster,
Johannes Gerrits (Van Vechten),
Marten Winnen,
Melchert Vanderpoel,
Elizabeth Kreigir,
Tryntje Wendell (now Millington),
Neeltje Schermerhorn (now Ten Eyck),
Elizabeth Ten Broek (now Coster),
Catrine Nack,
Geertruy Van Benthuysen (now Becker),
Maria Van der Poel (of Neoborum),
Cornelis (Indian),
Claas Jans.

October 25th, 1693.

Johannes Harmens (Visscher),
Moeset (Indian),
Marta do.
Sara do.
Jose do.

April 6th, 1694.

Pieter Hogenboom,
Johannes Kip,
Jacobus Van Schoonhoven,

Geertruy Van Schoonhoven,
Jecomintye Van Schoonhoven (now Van Deusen),
Geertje Willems,
Anna Bogardus,
Lydia Ten Broek,
Lysbeth Slingerlandt,
Christine Pruyn,
Catelyntje Schuyler (now Abeel),
Susanna Wendell,
Claartje Brott,
Elsje Hans,
Jannetje Swart (now Van der Zee),
Alida Fondaas (now Van Vechten),
Hester Fondas (wife of John Dircksen),
Lysbeth Jans,
Geertje Quakelbosch (now Groesbeck).

July 6th, 1694.

Gideon (Indian),
Alida do.

December 26th, 1694.

Neeltje Van Bergen (now Douw),
Dirk Van der Heyden,
David Schuyler,
Margriet (Indian),
Eva do.
Maria do.
Elsje do.

January 20th, 1695, of Kinderhook.

Arieentje Barents (wife of Pieter Martens),
Robbert Teuwis (Van Deusen),
Johannes Van Allen.

March 21st, 1695.

Thomas Harmens (Hun ?),
Hendrick Hans,
Tam Williams,
Agneetje Gansevoort (his wife),
Frans Winne,
Elsje Gansevoort (Winnen)
Claas Sivers,
Albert Rykman,
Gerrit Ryks,
Rachel Winne (of Schenectady),
Hendrik Pruyne,
Tryntje Cornelis (wife of Pieter Waldron),
Sara Foreest,
Claartje Quakelbosch (wife of Dirk Takelsen),
Annetje Hogenboom,
Rachel Slingerlandt,
Maria Wendell,
Dewertje Van Petten,
Anna Van Petten (wife of Claas Siversend),
Daniel Bratt,
Pieter (Indian),
Joseph do.
Tierk do.

Agniet (Indian),
Lea do.
Susanna do.
December 25th, 1695.
Cornelis Bogardus,
Brant (Indian),
Jacob do.
January 22d, 1696.
Jan Teuwis (Van Deusen),
Marrietje (Van Deusen),
Laurens Claas (Van Schaick,
Catelyntje Teuwis,
Jannetje Jochums (wife of Isaac Jans).
April 9th, 1696.
Myndert Rosenboom,
Abram Lansing,
Catrine Staat (now Schayk)
Saartje Brats (wife of Reynier Mynderts).
Anna Glen (now Wendell),
Maria Salisbury,
Mayken Van Esch (now Wendell),
Margreetje Pells,
Saartje Van Deusen,
June 26th, 1696.
Antonio (Indian),
Dorcas do.
Barent do.
Catrine do.
September 18th, 1696.
Johannes (Indian),
Arent do.
April 1st, 1697.
Mayken Van Esch (now Ouderkerck),
Annetje Schaats,
Margariet Ryks,
Elizbeth Lansing (now Groesbeck),
Susanna Wendell (now Wyngaard),
Margriet Schuyler (now Livingston),
Catrena Van Schayk (now Quakenbosch).
December 27th, 1697.
Sara Van Allen.
January 13th, 1698.
Guysbert Scharp,
Hendrik Jans (Witbeck),
Sara Jans (Witbeck),
Marritje Jans (Witbeck).
April 21st, 1698.
Hagar (Indian),
Jacomine do.
Luycas Lucas (Van Hoogkerke),
Solomon Cornels Van Vechten),
Hasuera Marselis,
Mars Ryks,
Harman Rykman,
Robbert Levingston, Jr.,
Margriet Levingston,
Margriet Van Trigt,
Margriet Blyker,
Margriet Harmens,
Catelina Wendell (now Schuyler),
Neeltje Gerrits,
Dirkje Winne,
Sara Marselis,

Marritje Roelofs (Kidni),
Helena Pruyn,
Lammertje Lokerman (Oothout).

January 8th, 1699, from Kinderhook.

Est Van Allen,
Stephenas Van Allen,
Manuel Van Schaack,
Lysbeth Arnoutse Van Eli.

April 6th, 1699.

Reyer Gerrits,
Jacobus Schuyler,
Andries Nack,
Hendrick Douw,
Jan Jans Van Aarnen,
Wouter Quakelbosch (married Cornelia, da. of Lawrence Bogert),
Matthyse Nak,
Maria Verplank,
Geertje Gerrits (Van den Bergh),
Lysbeth Gansevoort,
Margriet Rykman,
Lysbeth Viele (from Neoborum),
Helena Fonda,
Antje Quakelbosch,
Josina Maas (Van Buren ?),
Hillitje Gansevoort,
Maria Quakelbosch,
Neeltje Marinus,
Rachel Douw,
Cornelia Quakelbosch,
Anna Pruyn,
Canastasji (Indian).

September 8th, 1699.

Jonathan Braadhorst.

January 5th, 1700.

Susanna Wendells.

May 8th, 1700.

Claes Fonda,
Daniel Winnen,
Isack Ouderkerck,
Lysbet Wendell,
Mary Ingolsbie,
Rachel Bogardus,
Susanna Trujex.

NOTE F.

PETITIONS FOR THE INCORPORATION OF THE DUTCH CHURCH.

To the Honbl[e] Peter Schuyler Esqr President and the Rest of his Majesties Council of the province of New York and the Territories depending thereon in America.

The Humble Petition of Petrus van Driesen Minister of the Reformed Protestant Dutch Congregation in the City of Albany Joannis Cuyler Joannis Rooseboom Hendrick van Renslaer Willem Jacobse van Deusen present Elders for the same and Rutgert Bleecker Volkert van Veghten Myndert Roseboom and Dirk Ten Broek present Deacons of the said Church. Most Humbly Sheweth.

That the said Minister Elders and Deacons and other the members in Communion of the said Reformed Protestant Dutch Church have at their own charge built and erected a Church within the city of Albany and dedicated the same to the service of God, and have allso purchased Certain two Tenements and Lotts of ground for a Poor or alms house and for a minister's dwelling house; and sundry other small Tracts of Land within the said City the Rents and incomes whereof are by them (as they were allso by their Predecessors since they were Possessed of them) employed for the relief of the Poor and other Persons and charitable uses. And the Petitionrs further say that they and their predecessors have for many yeares before this Province was under the Government of the Crown of great Brittain and ever sinse Peaceably and quietly had and enjoyed the full and free Exercise of the Protestant Religion in the Dutch Language according to the Cannons Rules Instituсons and Church Government Established by the Nationall

Synod held and assembled in the City of Dort in Holland in the year 1618 and 1619.

And the Petitionrs humbly conceive and are advised that they and their Successors would be the better enabled to employ the Rents and incomes of the Lands and Tenement aforesaid for Pious and Charitable uses if they were incorporated as some other of the Protestant reformed Dutch Churches in this Province are.

They therefore most Humbly Pray yor Honors that the Peticonrs and their Successors may be Incorporated by Letters Patent under the great seal of this Province with such or the like Priviledges and Liberties as are granted to the Ministers Elders and Deacons of the Reformed Protestant Dutch Church in the City of New York and that the said Church and the aforesaid Tenements and Lotts of ground and other the Tracts and Parcells of Land aforesaid may be Confirmed unto them and their Successors for ever under such moderat Quit rent as unto yor Honors shall seem meet.

And yor Petitionrs as in Duty bound shall ever Pray &c—

PETRUS VAN DRIESEN
V D M
Nomine Synodij.

New York 3[d] day of August 1720.

To the Honble Peter Schuyler Esqr President and the Rest of his Majesties Councill of the Province of New York and the Territories depending thereon in America.

The Humble Petition of Petrus van Driesen Minister of the Dutch Protestant Congregacon in the City of Albany Joannis Cuyler Joannis Roseboom Hendrik van Renselaer and Willem Jacobse van Driesen the present Elders, Rutgert Bleeker Volckert van Vegten Myndert Roseboom and Dirk ten Broeck the present Deacons of the same—MOST HUMBLY SHEWETH

That yor Petitionrs did lately most humbly pray yor Honors to grant unto them and their Successors Letters Pattent under the Great Seal of this Province for incorporating them with such and the like Priviledges and Liberties as heretofore granted to the Reformed protestant Dutch Church in the City of New York together with a Confirmation of all such Lands and Tenements as they now hold to and for the use of the said Congregacon—

But so it is may it please yor Honors that one Mr Hendrik Hansen of the City of Albany has entered a Caveat against the passing of the said Patent under pretence that the Dutch Church erected in the City of Albany is built on some part of the ground belonging to the said Mr Hansen, and altho yor Petitionrs can easily make appear that the said pretence is groundless and only make up of by the said Hansen to delay yor Petitionrs in the Presenting and obtaining of the said Patent.

They therefore most Humbly Pray that for the Removing of all difficultyes and objections that may be raised against the passing of the said Patent a Clause may be inserted in the Same to save the Right and Title of all manner of persons to the Lands and Tenements or any part thereof which the Petitionrs by their former petition did Humbly pray to be Confirmed unto them and their Successors.

And yor Petitionrs as in duty bound shall ever Pray &c.

PETRUS VAN DRIESEN
V D M
Nomine Sijnodeii.

New York 6th Aug 1720

Act of Incorporation.

George by the grace of God King of Great Britain, France and Ireland, defender of the faith, &c., to all to whom these presents shall come or may concern, sendeth greeting: Whereas our loving subjects the Rev. Petrus Van Driessen, Johannes Cuyler, Johannes Rooseboom, Henrych Van Rensselaer, William Jacobse Van Deusen, Rutgert Bleecker, Volkert Van Veghten, Myndert Rooseboom and Dirck Tienbroock, the present ministers, elders and deacons of the Reformed Protestant Dutch Church in the city of Albany, in our province of New York, by their humble petition presented to our trusty and well beloved Colonel Peter Schuyler, president of our council for our province of New York, in council have set forth that the inhabitants of Albany, descended of Dutch ancestors, have from the first settlement of this province by Christians, hitherto held, used and enjoyed the free and undisturbed exercise of their religion and worship in the Dutch language, after the manner of the established Reformed Protestant religion in Holland, according to the common rules, institutions and church government of the national synod of Dort, in Holland, in the year of our Lord Christ one thousand six hundred and eighteen, and one thousand six hundred and nineteen. And that the said minister, elders and deacons, and their ancestors and predecessors, at their own charge and expense, erected, built and hitherto maintained a church within the city of Albany aforesaid, and have dedicated the same to the service and worship of Almighty God, situate, lying and being on the high street commonly called Yonkers street, nigh the bridge in the city of Albany, containing in length on the south side thereof seven rod, three foot four inches, on the north side seven rod three foot one inch, Ryland measure, and in breadth on the east and west ends, sixty-one foot and five inches, wood measure. And are now not only quietly and peaceably seized and possessed of their said church, but are likewise seized of sundry other demesnes to and for their sole and only proper use and behoof of their said church and congregation, that is to say, one certain messuage or tenement and lot of ground in the aforesaid city of Albany commonly called the Dutch minister's house, situate, lying and being in the Brewer's street, on the east side thereof, in the third ward of the said city, being in front from the southward to the northward five rod ten inches, and behind toward Hudson's river, six rod fifteen inches, Ryland measure, and in length from the said street to the city stockadoes, bounded on the south side by Jan Solomans, and on the north side by that of the late Hans Hendrycks and the widow of David Schuyler. Also one other certain messuage or tenement and lot of ground, situate, lying and being in the city aforesaid commonly called poor house or alms house, in the first ward of the said city, bounded on the south by the high street that leads to the burying place to the north of Rutten kill, and to the east of Harman Rutgers, and to the west by the lot of Garryt Bancker, containing in breadth towards the street that leads to the Lutheran church by the said Rutten kill, six rod one foot and the like breadth in the rear, and in length on the east side, eight rod and two inches, all Ryland measure. Also that certain parcel of land commonly called and known by the name of the pasture, situate, lying and being to the southward of the city of Albany, near the place where the old fort stood, extending along Hudson's river, till it comes over against the most northerly point of the island commonly called Marten Gerrytsen's island, having to the east Hudson's river, to the south the manor of Rensselaerswyck, to the west the highway that leads to the city aforesaid, the pastures now or late in the tenure and occupation of Martin Gerrytsen, and the pasture now or late in the tenure and occupation of Casper Jacobs, to the north the several pastures late in the tenure and occupation of Robert Saunders, Myndert Harmans and Evert Wendell, and the several gardens late in the occupation of Dirck Wessells, Killian Van Rensselaer and Abraham Staats, together with the old highway from Beaver kill to the end of Schermerhorn's pasture, adjoining to the same on the west side thereof. Also that certain parcel of pasture land situate, lying, and being to the southward of the said city, and to the westward of the before mentioned pasture, near and about the limits of the said city on the manor of Rensselaerswyck, containing in breadth along the wagon way, six and twenty rod, and in length towards the woods eight and twenty rod, and in breadth towards the woods twenty-five rod. And also all that certain garden lot of ground, situate, lying and being in the great pasture, containing in the breadth six rod and five foot, and in length eight rod and two foot, and stretching backwards with another small lot of three rod and two foot in length, and in breadth one rod and two foot Ryland measure; praying that they may by charter or patent under the great seal of the province of New York, be incorporated and made one body politic in fact and name, and that they and their successors forever hereafter, may not only be enabled to use, exercise and enjoy their aforesaid privileges, and the free use and exercise of their said religion and worship in manner aforesaid, by the name and style of the ministers, elders and deacons of the Reformed Protestant Dutch Church, in the city of Albany, with such other liberties and privileges as have been formerly granted to other Reformed Protestant Dutch churches within the province of New York, with variations, additions and commissions, as long usage and experience has taught them to be most agreeable to their well being and circumstances, but also the grant and confirmation of all those their said inheritances and demesnes, to hold to them, the said minister, elders and deacons of the Reformed Protestant Dutch Church in the city of Albany and to their successors and assigns for ever. We being willing to encourage and promote the said pious intentions and the free use and exercise of their said reformed protestant religion, to the same congregation and their successors for ever, in the said city of Albany, know ye, that of our especial grace, certain knowledge, and meer motion, we have given, granted, ratified, and confirmed and do by these presents for us, our heirs and successors for ever, give, grant, ratify, and confirm unto all the inhabitants of Albany, so as aforesaid descended of Dutch ancestors, and professing the said reformed protestant religion, and to their successors for ever, the free use and exercise of their worship, doctrine, discipline and church government, according to the canons, rules, institutions and directions of the Reformed Protestant Dutch Church in Holland, instituted and approved by the National Synod of Dort, and that no person nor persons whatsoever in communion of the said Reformed Protestant Dutch Church in Albany aforesaid, or at any time or times hereafter, shall be molested, disquieted, or disturbed in the free use and exercise of their said religion and worship, they behaving themselves peaceably, and not abusing this liberty to licentiousness, profaneness, and the civil injury or outward disturbance of the National Church of England, as by law established, or other reformed protestant churches in the aforesaid city of Albany. And to the end the same liberties and privileges be hereafter for ever supported, maintained, and continued to them and their successors for ever, we of our especial grace, certain knowledge and meer motion, do likewise will and grant for us, our heirs and successors for ever, unto the same Petrus Van Driessen, the present minister of the same congregation at Albany, Johannes Roseboom, Henryck Van Rensselaer, and William Jacobse Van Deusen, the present elders of the same church, and unto Rutgert Bleecker, Volkert Van Veghten, Myndert Roseboom, and Dirk Tienbroock, the present deacons of the same church, and the inhabitants of Albany communicants of the said church, that they be as they are hereby created and made one body corporate and politick in fact and name, by the name of the minister, elders and deacons of the Reformed Protestant Dutch Church in the city of Albany, and that they and their successors for ever, shall and may by that name have perpetual succession, and be able and capable in the law to sue and be sued, plead and be impleaded, answer and be answered unto, defend and be defended, in all and singular suit, quarrels, controversies, differences, strifes, matters and things whatsoever, and in all courts whatsoever, either in law or equity, of what kind soever, as also by the same name, to have, hold, take, receive, be seized of, possess and enjoy to them and their successors for ever their said church, parsonage or minister's dwelling-house, alms-house, and other their demesnes or inheritances, by fee simple, before mentioned, and such other demesnes or inheritances to purchase and acquire to them and their successors and assigns forever, and by the same name, the same lands, hereditaments and appurtenances, or any part of them (excepting only the same church); to alienate, bargain, sell, grant, demise, sell and to farm let to any other person, or persons, body corporate and politic, whatsoever at their will and pleasure, in fee simple for life, or lives, or for term of years, as to them shall seem most convenient and profitable, as any other person or persons, body corporate or politic, may or can do, not exceeding the yearly value of three hundred pounds over and above what they now stand seized and possessed, or for the common use and benefit of the same Dutch Church and of all the members of the same congregation. And we do further will and grant that the minister, elders and deacons of the same church, for the time being, for ever hereafter, be the consistory of the same church, and shall and may have, keep and use a common seal to serve for all grants, matters and things whatsoever belonging to the same corporation, with such device or contrivance thereon as they or their successors for ever shall think fit to appoint, with full power to break, new make and alter the same at their will and discretion; and the same consistory shall have and enjoy the like powers and privileges as a Dutch consistory in the Reformed Protestant Dutch Church in Holland do, or may or ought to use and enjoy. And we do will and grant that the same Petrus Van Driessen be the first minister of the said church at the time of this our grant, and the same Johannes Cuyler, Johannes Roseboom, Henryck Van Rensselaer and William Jacobse Van Deusen, be the first elders of the said church at the time of this our grant; and that the same Rutgert Bleecker, Volkert Van Veghten, Myndert Roseboom, and Dirk Tienbroock, be the first deacons of the said church at the time of this our grant, to all intents and purposes; and that the said ministers, together with the said four elders and four deacons, or the minister, elders and deacons for the time being, and the major numbers of them whereof the minister for the time being always to be one—be the consistory of the said church, and have and shall have full power and authority, at all time and times for ever hereafter, to act in all their church affairs and business, by majority of voices, in as full and ample manner as if the minister and all the said four elders and four deacons were personally present and did actually and severally give their votes. But in case of the death, absence or removal of their said minister, then, and in any of these cases, the elders and deacons of the same church, for the time being, or the major number of them, whereof the first elder in nomination we will always to be one, and shall preside, shall have, use and exercise all the power and authorities of a consistory to all intents and purposes, and shall manage and order the church affairs in as full and ample manner as if their said minister were alive, present and consenting thereunto, any thing in these presents to the contrary thereof in any wise notwithstanding. And we will and grant that the same elders and deacons continue in their respective offices until the next anniversary election. And the said elders and their successors, for ever hereafter, have and shall have the full power and authority of receiving and paying the moneys given for the maintenance of the minister or ministry of the same church, whether the same arise by legacy, donation or voluntary contributions or collection from the inhabitants or members of the same congregation, and are to keep exact and true accounts to the consistory, when thereunto by them required. And that the said deacons and their successors for ever hereafter, have and shall have the sole power and authority of receiving and paying all the moneys collected and offered at the administration of the Holy Sacrament of our Lord's Supper, and in church in the times of divine service of preaching, for the maintainance of the poor, and are to keep and render exact and true accounts thereof to the consistory aforesaid, when thereunto by them required, which election of the same elders and deacons of the same church is to be at Albany on every second Saturday of December, annually, forever, by majority of voices, of the consistory, in the manner following: That is to say, on each second Saturday of December, annually for ever at Albany, shall be chosen two new elders and two new deacons, who, together with the two elders and two deacons last in nomination in this our charter, shall serve for the year ensuing in their respective offices, and for ever thereafter, the two new ones shall be chosen and added to the younger two elders and deacons of the preceding year, so always as to preserve the number of four elders and four deacons of the said church. And moreover we do will and grant unto the said minister, elders and deacons of the Reformed Protestant Dutch Church in the city of Albany, and to their successors for ever, that on the second Saturday of December next, and on every second Saturday of December annually forever hereafter at Albany, shall be elected and chosen four discreet persons by the majority of voices of the consistory aforesaid, to be kirkmasters of the said church, whose office and charge is and shall be to build and repair the same church and cemetery, parsonage, almshouse, and all other the hereditaments and appurtenances to the said church belonging, and to have the ordering and direction of the pews and seats in the said church, and the breaking of the ground in the cemetery for burying of the dead, and shall have and receive all the rents and revenues of the said church, coming therefrom or from any other of the said church's inheritances; also the payments of all sum and sums of money laid out and expended, or to be laid out and expended, in such necessary buildings and reparations of all which the said kirkmasters are likewise to keep and surrender exact and true accounts to the said consistory aforesaid, two of which four kirkmasters last nominated, at the next election shall continue in the same office for two years and two new ones yearly for ever hereafter, to be elected and chosen to serve with the two predecessors in like manner as with the elders and deacons aforesaid and not otherwise. And it is our will and desire that the two elders, two deacons and two kirkmasters, who shall be superseded by a new annual election of two others to succeed in their respective places, shall account and deliver up their several respective charges and moneys to their successors respectively, if any thereof be in their hands and possession, respectively in public manner. And we do likewise will and grant that the said kirkmasters shall be under the direction of the said consistory for the time being. And in case there shall not be enough in the hands either of the elders, deacons or kirkmasters, for the performing and finishing of any of their respective charges and trust of their particular respective funds before mentioned, which they be hereby respectively empowered to receive and manage, that then it shall and may be lawful to and for the consistory aforesaid, to order and direct the lending of what sum shall be necessary out of any of the aforesaid funds towards deficiency of any other of the said funds, so that there be no failure of any of the same three several charges or trusts upon any unforeseen contingency or emergency. And we do likewise will and grant that in all elections of officers or other acts or orders of the consistory the minister or president of the consistory shall have but one vote. And if it shall happen there be an equal division of the voices or votes, so that the matter or thing in dispute can not receive the determination of a majority of voices, that then it shall and may be lawful to determine the same by lot, leaving it to the sole wisdom of God to determine the same as he shall think fit. And we do likewise will and grant that it shall be in the power of the minister of the said church, for the time being, by himself or in case of his death, absence or removal, in the president or first elder who shall preside for the time being, or in the power of the major number of the whole consistory for the time being, to call a meeting of the consistory for the good and service of the said church, and the affairs of the said corporation, whensoever they shall see meet within the said city of Albany; and in case it shall please God that any of the said elders, deacons and kirkmasters, for the time being, shall happen to die, remove, or otherwise be disabled from serving and officiating in their respective offices, within the year for which they are so chosen or appointed to serve; we do will and grant that it shall and may be lawful to the consistory, for the time being, to assemble and meet together at Albany, at any other time of the year than the time of anniversary election, and so often as there shall be occasion to elect and choose other elders, deacons and kirkmasters in their respective rooms and stead, to officiate for the remaining part of the year until the next anniversary election; which person or persons so chosen as aforesaid into any of the aforesaid offices of elders, deacons or kirkmasters, shall have like power and authority to act in their respective offices as if they had been elected and confirmed at the aforesaid time of the anniversary election aforesaid, or as if the same persons so dying, being absent or otherwise disabled, were alive, present and capable to do the same; and we do will and grant unto the said minister, elders and deacons of the Reformed Protestant Dutch Church in the city of Albany, and to their successors for ever, the advowson and patronage of the said church; (that is to say) that after the decease of the aforesaid Petrus Van Driessen, or next and all other avoidances thereof, that it shall and may be lawful to and for the elders and deacons of the aforesaid church or the consistory of the aforesaid church and their successors for ever, to present and call another minister to succeed in the cure of souls in the aforesaid church and congregation of the Reformed Protestant Dutch Church in the city of Albany, provided always such minister, so called or presented by them to the said living, be always a person amenable to the laws of Great Britain and this Province, and pay due obedience and allegiance unto us and our royal heirs and successors, the kings and queens of Great Britain. And that it shall and may be lawful to and for the present minister or incumbent of the said church and his succesors, or any of them to have, take, receive and keep for his end and their own use and support, that maintenance that now is or shall be agreed upon between him or them and the said consistory from time to time, and at all times hereafter. And it shall and may be lawful to and for the said elders of the same church, and their successors for ever, to collect and receive the voluntary subscriptions of the inhabitants of Albany, belonging to the said congregation, for and towards the payment of their said minister, or their minister for the time being, and to pay and cause to be paid unto the said minister and his successor, the minister of the said church, for the time being, his yearly stipend or salary, according to agreement, by quarterly even payments thereof, or otherwise, as it shall be agreed upon by and between them, the said minister of the said church and the aforesaid consistory. And we do will and grant that the said deacons of the said church, and their successors for ever shall and may lawfully and peaceably, from time to time, and at all times hereafter, at the meeting of the said congregation for the public service and worship of Almighty God, to collect and receive the free and voluntary alms and oblations of the members of the said congregation, and the free and voluntary offerings made by the communicants at their receiving of the holy sacrament of the Lord's Supper for the uses aforesaid, and to dispose thereof for the pious and charitable uses aforesaid.

And we do will and grant that the kirkmasters aforesaid, and their successors for ever, shall and may from time to time, and at all times hereafter, and so often as it shall be necessary, shall and may demise, grant, and to farm let, of the demesnes of the said church, demisable and grantable to and for the profit and advantage of the said church, and receive and collect the rents and revenues arising therefrom, or otherwise, and apply the same for and towards the buildings and reparations of the said church and parsonage, and other the hereditaments belonging to the said minister, elders and deacons of the Reformed Protestant Dutch Church in the city of Albany, and such other uses as are proper and necessary, provided always that the said elders, deacons and kirkmasters in their separate offices, be always accountable to and under the direction of the consistory of the said church, for the time being and not otherwise. And we do further will and grant that it shall and may be in the power of the consistory of the said church, and their successors for ever, if they shall agree thereupon, and find themselves able and capable of mantaining him at any time or times hereafter, to nominate and call one or more able and sufficient minister, lawfully ordained according to the constitution aforesaid, in all things to assist and officiate in the ministry which doth belong to the sacred office and function of a minister of the gospel in the said church, provided always that there be no pre-eminency or superiority in that office, and not otherwise. And we do likewise will and grant to the said minister, elders, and deacons of the Reformed Protestant Dutch Church in the city of Albany, and their successors for ever, that it shall and may be lawfull to and for the consistory of the said church, to nominate and appoint a clerk or precentor, schoolmaster, sexton, bellringer, and such and so many other offices and servants of the same church, as they shall think convenient and necessary, and to call them, by the same or what other names they shall think fit. And we do will and grant that it shall and may be lawfull to and for the consistory of the said church, and their successors from time to time, and at all times hereafter, to make rules, orders, and ordinances for the better discipline and government of the said church, provided always that such rules, orders and ordinances shall not be binding, nor effect any other of our reformed protestant subjects within the same city, then the voluntary members of their said congregation, and be no ways repugnant to our laws of Great Britain and of this colony, but agreeable to the articles of faith and worship agreed upon and instituted by the National Synod at Dort, aforesaid. And further of our especial grace, certain knowledge and meer motion, we have given, granted, ratified, and confirmed unto the aforesaid minister, elders, and deacons of the Reformed Protestant Dutch Church in the city of Albany, and to their successors and assigns for ever, all that their said church and ground whereon it standeth, their said parsonage or minister's dwelling house, with its hereditaments and appurtenances thereunto belonging or any ways appertaining, and all the alms house or poor house aforesaid, all that the pasture or pastures, and all other the premises aforesaid, together with all and singular edifices, buildings, gardens, orchards, backsides, wells, ways, hollows, cellars, passages, privileges, liberties, profits, advantages, hereditaments, and appurtenances whatsoever, to all and every of them belonging, or in any ways appertaining. And all that our estate, right, title, interest, property and demand of, into or out of the same or any part of any of them, and the revertions, remainders, and the yearly rents and profits of the same, saving only the right and title of any other person or persons, body corporate and politick whatsoever, to any of the premises hereby granted, or meant, mentioned, and intended to be hereby granted, or to any of them, to have and to hold, all that their said church and ground, parsonage or minister's dwelling house, alms house or poor house, pasture or pastures, and all and singular other the premises with their and every of their hereditaments and appurtenances unto the aforesaid minister, elders and deacons of the Reformed Protestant Dutch Church in the city of Albany, their successors and assigns for ever, to the sole and only proper use, benefit and behoof of the aforesaid minister, elders and deacons of the Reformed Protestant Dutch Church, in the city of Albany, and their successors and assigns for ever (save only as before is saved and expressed), to be holden of us, our heirs and successors for ever, free and common soccage as of our manor of East Greenwich, in the county of Kent, within our realm of Great Britain, yielding, rendering and paying therefore, yearly and every year, for ever unto us, our heirs and successors for ever, at our custom house in New York, unto our and their receiver general for the time being, on the feast day of the Annunciation of the Blessed Virgin Mary, commonly called Lady Day, the annual rent of one pepper corn, if the same be lawfully demanded in lieu and stead of all other rents, services, dues and duties and demands whatsoever, for the same church parsonage, alms house, pastures, and all other the above granted premises, with the hereditaments and appurtenances. And we do hereby will and grant unto the aforesaid minister, elders and deacons of the Reformed Protestant Dutch Church in the city of Albany, and to their successors for ever, that these our letters shall be made patent, and that they and the record of them remaining in our secretary's office of our province of New York, shall be good and effectual in the law to all intents and purposes whatsoever, according to the true intent and meaning of them, and shall be construed, reputed, esteemed and adjudged in all cases most favorable for the benefit and behoof of the aforesaid minister, elders and deacons of the Reformed Protestant Dutch Church in the city of Albany and of their successors forever, notwithstanding the not true and well reciting of the premises, or of the limits and bounds of any of them, or any part of them, any law or other restraint, uncertainty or imperfection whatsoever to the contrary thereof in any way notwithstanding. In testimony whereof we have caused the great seal of our province of New York to be affixed to these presents, and the same to be entered of record in one of the books of patents in our said secretary's office remaining. Witness our said trusty and well beloved Colonel Peter Schuyler, president of our council at Fort George, the 10th day of August, in the 7th year of our reign, anno domini 1720.

Causes and History of the Separation.

A brief sketch of the causes and history of the separation may be interesting to the reader.

Up to 1737, the churches in this country were all connected with the ecclesiastical courts in Holland, and were under their jurisdiction. The inconveniences of this connection now began to be seriously felt, and openly discussed. The highest church court here was only the consistory, consequently there could be no ordination of ministers. All candidates were obliged to go to Holland to receive ordination, incurring a large expenditure of time and money. No case of discipline could be settled here, for the ultimate tribunals were on the other side of the ocean. Congregations were a long time without pastors. And in some cases the ministers who were sent out from Holland were unsuitable persons for the churches here.

The first movement was the formation of what was called a cœtus, which was a body formed for counsel and fraternal conference. It was merely an advisory body, and had no legislative powers. They applied to the classis of Amsterdam to sanction their organization, which after a delay of nine years was done in 1747.

It was however found that this body was powerless to remove the evils under which the American churches suffered, by reason of their dependence on the fatherland, and in 1754 it was formally proposed that the cœtus should be made a regular classis, with all the powers appropriately belonging to such a court. This was bitterly opposed by many of the older ministers, who had been ordained in Holland, and who looked upon the proposed separation as treason to the mother Church. A bitter dispute arose, and raged for fifteen years. The party which opposed the separation were called the Conferentie, the other the Cœtus. These two parties carried on a controversy of the most determined character, which disturbed the peace of neighborhoods, divided families, and rent the churches into factions. Houses of worship were locked up, ministers were assaulted in the discharge of their functions, and the holy sabbath was profaned by scenes of violence and mobs.

Such was the sad state of things when Dr. John H. Livingston in 176– went to Holland to study theology, and be ordained to the work of the ministry. By judicious personal conference with the clergy of Holland he disarmed their prejudices, and gave them correct views of the wants of the Church in America. He then obtained the consent of the synod of North Holland that the classis of Amsterdam should have in its charge all the matters relating to the American churches. He then returned to this country, was settled in New York, and soon after called a convention of ministers and elders, which met in that city in October, 1771, and of which he was chosen president. The convention conducted their deliberations in a fraternal, and candid spirit. The result was the formation of a plan of union, which provided: 1st. For the internal arrangement and government of the churches, the organization of superior church courts, the establishment of a professorship for the education of ministers, and for the foundation of schools. 2d. For the healing of dissensions in the various churches. 3d. For correspondence with the Church in Holland. It was provided that the minutes of the ecclesiastical courts should always be sent to the classis of Amsterdam, and that the classis, or if need be the synod of North Holland, might be appealed to in cases of difficulty.

This plan was cordially adopted, sent to the classis of Amsterdam, and by them approved. Their letter of approbation, expressed in the most cordial terms, and breathing an excellent spirit, was read in convention in October, 1772, and peace was at last restored to the American churches.

NOTE G.

Distinguished individuals who have been at different times connected with the congregation of the Reformed Protestant Dutch Church of Albany.

Abraham Yates, Jr.

Before the commencement of the Revolutionary war, Mr. Yates had obtained a distinguished and extensive reputation as a patriot. While sheriff of the city and county of Albany, he resisted the quartering of troops upon its citizens, and was threatend with arrest by the government for so doing. He was the author of a series of letters signed Rough Hewer, which had an extensive circulation, and exercised an influence second only to the famous articles, entitled *Common Sense*, in giving character and direction to public sentiment. He was chairman of the committee of public safety, during part of the Revolutionary war, a member of the convention which formed the first constitution of the state, recorder and mayor of the city of Albany, and held other offices of trust and distinction.

HON. ROBERT YATES.

He was a cousin of Hon. Abraham Yates, Jr., and a man of note in his day. He was a delegate to the convention which formed the constitution of the United States. In 1777, he was appointed one of the first justices of the supreme court of New York, and in 1790, became chief justice of the same. He was a man of great intellectual power, and largely contributed to the success of our struggle for national independence.

SAMUEL STRINGER, M. D.

Dr. Stringer, was a man of great eminence in the profession of medicine, and ranked among the first practitioners of his day. He was also an ardent patriot. He was chairman of the committee of public safety in this city during a part of the Revolutionary war, and was also surgeon general of the forces under Gen. Schuyler, during that memorable struggle. A man of fine education, distinguished professional abilities, ardent zeal in behalf of the cause of his country, great dignity of manners, and gentlemanliness of deportment, he deservedly commanded high respect, and occupied a very prominent place in public estimation. He died in 1818.

Brig. Gen. Peter Gansevoort.

Gen. Gansevoort's name is identified honorably with the history of his country. He was born in Albany, July 16th, 1749, and educated in New Jersey. In 1775, he was appointed by congress a major in the second regiment of New York, and joined the expedition under Gen. Montgomery. In 1776, he received a colonel's commission in the third regiment of the army of the United States. In 1777, he commanded Fort Stanwix during its memorable siege, and conducted its defence with a vigor and success which crowned his name with distinguished honor, and for which he received a special vote of thanks from congress. In 1809, he received the commission of brigadier general in the army of the United States, in which service he continued till his death, which occurred 2d of July, 1812, in the 63d year of his age.

He was a man of noble presence, and fearless and magnanimous spirit; of undaunted courage, and inflexible integrity. His public life was without a blot, while his private character was of unimpeachable morality, and showed distinctly the influence of Christian principle.

Hon. Leonard Gansevoort.

He was the brother of Gen. Gansevoort. Much of his life was spent in commercial pursuits, in which he always maintained a high position as an enterprising and honorable merchant. He was also a devoted patriot. He was president of the convention which adopted the first constitution of this state, in April, 1777, and was the first judge of probate in the county of Albany, which office he held for many years. The later portion of his life was spent at Whitehall, his country seat, in the vicinity of Albany, where he ever displayed the dignified, and generous hospitality characteristic of those days. He was a devoted member of this church, and sat as a ruling elder in her councils, for many years.

Hon. Simeon DeWitt.

Mr. DeWitt was born Dec. 25th, 1756, in Ulster county. He was educated at Queens (now Rutgers) college, where he took high rank as a scholar, and at his graduation received the double honor of the salutatory, and valedictory orations. At the time of the incursion of Burgoyne he joined the army, and was present at the battle in which that distinguished general was defeated, and witnessed his surrender. In 1778, he was appointed assistant geographer (or as it would now be called, topographical engineer), to the army, and in 1780, on the death of the chief geographer, Col. Robert Erskine, he succeeded to that honorable and important post. He was attached to the main army from 1780 to the close of the war, was present at the siege of Yorktown, and witnessed the surrender of Cornwallis. In 1784, he was appointed surveyor general of the state of New York, and held this commission more than fifty years. In 1796, Gen. Washington, with whom Mr. DeWitt was on terms of cordial intimacy, without his knowledge or solicitation, nominated him to the senate, as surveyor general of the United States, which was cordially ratified by that body. This flattering appointment Mr. DeWitt did not feel at liberty to accept. In 1798, he was elected a regent; in 1817, vice chancellor; and in 1829, chancellor of the University of New York. He was a member of various literary and scientific associations, and frequently made valuable contributions with his pen to the progress of scientific inquiry. He was distinguished for his habits of close study, and persevering investigation. He was a true philosopher with all the treasures, but without any pride of learning. His official life was useful to his country, and honorable to himself. And in the social relations of life he was warm in his affections, and firm and true in his friendships.

Mr. DeWitt was a sincere and exemplary Christian. For more than twenty years, he was a ruling elder in the Protestant Reformed Dutch Church in this city. At the division of the Church, in 1815, he became connected with the Second Dutch Church, where his children still remain, and where his memory is yet precious, as the memory of the just. He died on the 3d of December, 1834, within a few days of accomplishing his 79th year.

Hon. John Lansing, Jr.

Mr. Lansing was one of the most prominent jurists of his day. After practicing law with signal ability and success for a number of years, he was appointed in 1790 a judge of the supreme court of this state, of which in 1798, he was made chief justice. In 1801, he was made chancellor, which high office he filled with distinguished ability. He was mayor of the city of Albany from 1786 to 1790. In all his public offices he united with great professional talent, an irreproachable moral character, and commanded the respect and confidence of his fellow citizens.

Hon. Abraham Van Vechten.

Few names are held in such respectful remembrance by the citizens of Albany as the name of Mr. Van Vechten. He was born at Catskill, December 5th, 1752, and educated at the Kingston Academy. His progress in learning was so remarkable that he was able at the early age of fourteen, to commence the study of law with chancellor Lansing of this city, and was actually licensed both as attorney and counselor, before he was twenty-one years of age. He commenced practice in this city in 1793. He was soon after elected to the senate of the state, and for nearly thirty years, held a seat in one of the two branches of the legislature. For eleven years he was recorder of the city of Albany; was appointed attorney general of the state in 1811, and was more than once invited to a seat on the bench of the supreme court, which honor he declined.

He made a profession of religion about the time he commenced professional life, and was for more than half a century, an active, consistent, and useful member of the Church. He was often an elder and a member of our ecclesiastical courts, in which he always exerted great influence.

Mr. Van Vechten was a man of vigorous intellect, sound judgment, and remarkable discrimination. His learning, particularly in jurisprudence, was various, thorough and extensive. In his disposition he was generous and benevolent, simple in his habits, warm in his affections, frank and easy in his manners. He was a sincere and exemplary Christian. He loved the Bible, and prayer, and the ordinances of the house of God. He was devotedly attached to the Dutch Church, and no man in the long list of her members deserves to be more gratefully remembered by that Church.

Hon. Harmanus Bleecker.

Mr. Bleecker was the fifth in descent from Jan Jansen Bleecker, who was one of the early settlers in Albany, and who married, in 1667, Margaret, daughter of Rutger Jacobsen. He was born October 9th, 1779; was admitted to the bar in 1801; and in 1810 was elected to congress where he served during the troublous times of the last war with England. He was one of the regents of the university, and a commissioner on the part of the state, for settling the boundary between New York and New Jersey. Under the administration of president Van Buren, he was sent as American minister to the Hague. Very few of our foreign ministers have made such a favorable impression abroad. During his residence in Holland he married Miss Sebastiana Cornelia Mentz, an accomplished lady, who still survives him in her native land.

Mr. Bleecker was a man of uncommon literary attainments and high cultivation. He was dignified in his manners, and affable and courteous in his deportment. He spoke and wrote in the Dutch language with great purity and elegance, and was on this account very popular during his residence abroad. He was a man of irreproachable character, a consistent supporter of the institutions of religion, and more than usually versed in the science of theology. He died at his residence in Albany, July 19th, 1849, at the age of seventy years.

Hon. Stephen Van Rensselaer.

This is one of the most precious names connected with the Church of Albany. Mr. Van Rensselaer was born in the city of New York, November 1st, 1764, and graduated at Harvard University in 1782. In 1789, he was chosen to the legislature of this state, and in 1795, when only thirty-one years of age, was called to preside over the senate as lieutenant governor. He held this position six years. From 1800 to 1820, he was frequently a member of assembly, sat in two conventions called to revise the constitution, and in 1822 was elected to the congress of the United States. For the last fourteen years of his life he was president of the canal board, and at the time of his death, was chancellor of the University of New York.

He began his military career in 1787, and during the last war with Great Britain he held the commission of major general, commanded on the Niagara frontier, and was engaged with honor in the battle of Queenstown.

In 1825, he received from Yale College the honorary degree of doctor of laws. He died suddenly at the Manor House, January 26th, 1839.

The following extract from a discourse delivered in his memory by his eloquent and intimate friend, Rev. George W. Bethune, D. D., at Philadelphia, February 3d, 1839, contains a just analysis of his character, and tribute to his worth.

"Born to a large patrimony, the increasing prosperity of the country poured wealth upon him, until he became, with the exception, perhaps, of one other, the richest man of the land; and wearing, by the common consent of all around him, the only hereditary title known among us, he swayed an influence wider than any other private citizen possessed. Cautious, but not cold; frank, but never rash; without the qualities of fervid genius, or depth of learning, he had a judgment singularly clear and correct, a pure common sense, which rarely failed to guide him in duties which his conscience loved. Surrounded by grateful dependents and affectionate friends, though there could not be wanting those who would have preyed upon his abounding fortunes, he has gone to his grave without an enemy.

"The beauty of his wisdom was his guilelessness, the strength of his power was his goodness, and the abundance of his wealth his vast benevolence.

"His greatness was like that of a noble tree, planted by the river of the water of life, spreading wide its sheltering arms to overshadow all who needed refuge, which yielded perennial fruits, and "whose leaf never faded." His bounty was not the occasional and noisy gushes of ostentatious pride, but silent, secret, and gentle as the dew, refreshing far and near, yet with a kindly care for the lowliest herb of the field, healing but never wounding the heart it blessed; while every drop glistened in the light of the Sun of Righteousness, and was exhaled to heaven. * * * *

"An elder in the church of his fathers, he seemed to count it his best honor to serve the followers of Jesus; and when a member of ecclesiastical courts, as he frequently was, he never shrank from any labor, nor became "weary in well doing." It may be safely said, that the church he so much loved, approaching as it does, more nearly than any other, the order of the apostolic age, became dearer, and yet dearer to his heart as he drew near his end.

"Yet sect could not confine the charity of his spirit. We dare not claim him as wholly our own. He belonged to Christianity, to the world, because he belonged to God and Christ; and never was his aid sought in any cause of benevolence, morals or piety (and the applications were as constant as the day, and numerous as its hours,) that his answer was not that of "the cheerful giver" whom "the Lord loves."

"But it was in his home that the Christian shone most radiantly and sweetly, where his gentle spirit found delightful fellowship with the innocence of children, and the quiet loveliness of kindred affection. The guest, who crossed that threshold, forgot he was a stranger, and though poor, amidst all the appliances of uncounted wealth, felt only that he was at home. Alas! for the bereaved hearts within that dwelling which knows him now no more! God comfort them!

"Long suffering had chastened his spirit to an almost heavenly purity, and they, who "marked the perfect, and beheld the upright," saw, that "the end of that man was peace." In the midst of his affectionate children and near his devoted wife, within the hall where the servant of God, and the friend of man, ever found an unfeigned welcome, his venerable head fell gently upon his bosom. He was asleep in Jesus. His flesh shall rest in hope, but his spirit is now singing the song in heaven he loved to sing on earth. He "rests from his labors, and his works have followed him."

HON. KILIAN K. VAN RENSSELAER.

Mr. Van Rensselaer was the son of Kilian Van Rensselaer, Esq., of Greenbush. His father was at one time chairman of the general committee of safety for the northern department of New York, in the Revolutionary war. Three of the sons served as commissioned officers in that war, and two of them were severely wounded in different engagements.

He was educated for the legal profession, in which he for many years held a high rank in this city. He served for several years in the city councils, and about 1800, was elected to congress. He retained his seat for five successive terms and was always distinguished for his intelligence, his decision of character, his integrity, and the urbanity of his manners.

He was for many years a member of this Church, and was often elected to a seat in consistory.

He died June 18th, 1845, at the age of 82, having always enjoyed the esteem and confidence of his fellow citizens, and leaving behind him a spotless memory. Three of his sons still survive him, and are among the most respectable citizens of Albany; one of them, Gen. John S. Van Rensselaer, being the father of the gallant and lamented Charles M. Van Rensselaer, first officer of the ill-fated steamer Central America.

Maj. Gen. Solomon Van Rensselaer.

Gen. Van Rensselaer, was the son of Gen. Henry R. Van Rensselaer of Revolutionary memory, and was born August 6th, 1774. He joined the army before he was eighteen years of age, under Gen. Anthony Wayne. His gallantry at that early age was conspicuous, and his promotion was rapid, so that he commanded a troop before he had reached the age of twenty. In the battle of the Miami, in 1794, he was shot through the lungs, and almost by miracle survived the wound. After the disbanding of the army he was appointed adjutant general of this state under Gov. Jay, which post he held for a number of years. During the last war he was aid to Maj. Gen. Stephen Van Rensselaer on the Niagara frontier, and rendered brilliant and effective service throughout the campaign. At the battle of Queenstown he received six balls in different parts of his body, one of which he carried to the day of his death.

In 1818 he was elected to congress, and at the expiration of his term of office was re-elected. Under President Monroe he was appointed postmaster of Albany, and held this office under Adams and Jackson. In 1839, he was a delegate to the national convention at Harrisburgh, which nominated Gen. Harrison for the presidency. From President Harrison he received again the appointment of postmaster at Albany. The last years of his life were spent in the bosom of his affectionate family at Cherry Hill, where he died April 23d, 1852, in the 78th year of his age, leaving behind him the memory of a gallant soldier, a true patriot, and a faithful servant of his country.

Abraham G. Lansing, Esq.

The estimation in which Mr. Lansing was held by the public may be well inferred from the following obituary notice from the pen of his distinguished friend, Abraham Van Vechten, Esq., which appeared in the Albany Argus, September, 1834.

"It is due to the memory of those who have well performed their part on the stage of life, that their example should be held forth for imitation after their departure hence ; for in this way it furnishes a useful lesson to their survivors. The recent death of Abraham G. Lansing, Esq., at the advanced age of 77 years, affords such a lesson.

"Mr. Lansing was a native of this city, and a zealous and active supporter of the liberties of our country during the American Revolution. His merit and patriotism at an early period attracted the attention and engaged the confidence of our distinguished leaders in that arduous contest, who confided to him several important offices, the duties of which he discharged with faithfulness and ability. After the war of our independence was ended, Mr. Lansing received appointments to various responsible public offices, from the United States, as well as from this state, in all of which he merited and preserved the undiminished confidence and esteem of his fellow citizens. Happy in his domestic relations, with an amiable and interesting family, who delighted to minister to his comfort and happiness, he led a life of benevolence and usefulness, and died in the faith and hope of a humble Christian, and is buried in the affections of his bereaved wife, children, and friends."

Hon. Charles E. Dudley.

The name of Mr. Dudley, already distinguished by his own character and public services, has been rendered still more extensively so, by the noble monument, which the affection and munificence of his widow has reared to his memory, and on which she has inscribed his name in letters as bright as the stars to which it points.

Descended from one of the most ancient of the noble families of England, Mr. Dudley was thoroughly and deeply attached to this country, the land of his adoption, and of his life and labors. After engaging for years in the honorable and useful pursuits of commercial life, in which he was very successful, he retired to Albany, and became happily connected in marriage with one of its most ancient and respectable families. He was soon called to preside over the municipal government of the city; thence he was transferred to the senate of the state, where "he identified his name with beneficent measures, which have contributed largely to the intellectual progress and material prosperity of the state." He was afterward elected to the senate of the United States, and in that body, which was then illuminated by those brilliant stars, Clay, Webster, and Calhoun, and Silas Wright, his distinguished colleague, he shone with no ordinary lustre. Intelligence, candor, patriotism, and independence, characterized his course as a statesman, no less than his character as a man.

"It was his fortune," says Gov. Hunt, in his address at the inauguration of the Dudley Observatory, "to act a prominent part on the stage of public events in times of intense political excitement. Though decided in his opinions, adhering always to his avowed principles with unyielding firmness, party spirit never ventured to assail the integrity of his conduct, or to question the purity of his intentions. He cherished warm political attachments, yet he was no partisan, in the ordinary sense. If he loved Cæsar much, he loved Rome more, and regarded the welfare of his country as paramount to the interests of any party." His long acquaintance with commerce, and knowledge of the laws of trade, gave him peculiar advantages on questions which related to the commercial interests of the country; and his views on these subjects always commanded a larger measure of consideration.

From the period of his marriage, Mr. Dudley was a regular worshiper in the Dutch Church, in connection with which he remained during the remainder of his life. He was a man who had a sincere reverence for the institutions of religion, and his moral character was above reproach. He professed his faith in Christ in his last illness, and the hopes of the gospel cheered him in his dying hours. He was dignified and courteous in his manners, and commanded the respect of the public as truly as he won the affection of his friends.

He died in Albany in 1841. His affectionate widow still survives him, herself the descendant of one of the first magistrates of the city, and one of the oldest members of the Dutch Church of Albany. Through her lamented husband and herself, the name of Dudley will be rendered memorable, when centuries hence, the astronomer shall watch the stars which look down upon their graves in silent and solemn beauty.

Rev. William J. Pohlman.

Mr. Pohlman was born in Albany February 17th, 1812. He was trained up by pious parents in the nurture, and admonition of the Lord, and was the subject of deep religious impressions from his earliest years. When he was about 16 years of age he became a decided Christian, and eighteen months after, he connected himself with this Church. Feeling then an ardent desire to devote himself to the Gospel ministry, he commenced a course of preparatory study, passed through Rutgers College and the theological seminary, and was duly licensed to preach by the Rev. Classis of Albany, July 27th, 1837. He now determined to devote himself to the foreign missionary work, and applied to the American Board of Commissioners for Foreign Missions to be employed by them on heathen ground. His application was cordially granted, and in April, 1838, he was ordained in this Church to the work of the ministry. On the 20th of May, 1838, he was solemnly set apart to the work of foreign missions, and immediately left for the island of Borneo, which was designated as the field of his labors. In 1844, he was transferred to the mission at Amoy, in China, where he labored with zeal and fidelity for about five years. In January 1849, while passing from Hong Kong to Amoy, the vessel in which he sailed encountered a severe storm, in which she foundered, and Mr. Pohlman was among the lost.

The Rev. Dr. Kennedy, who was at that time pastor of this Church, and who knew Mr. Pohlman well, in a discourse delivered in his memory in May, 1849, says of him, that he "possessed elements of character, that fitted him for extended usefulness among the heathen. His piety took the form of a deep controlling principle. It governed him in every thing he did. Were I to select what seems to me to have been the prominent feature of his mental constitution, I would say it was *perseverance.* And the union of these two elements, *deep piety*, and *unwearying perseverance*, gave a cast to the entire character, and fitted him in an eminent degree for the toils and trials of the missionary life. Difficulties never discouraged him. Obstacles only nerved him to greater exertions. He was cheerful in duty, prudent in counsel, amiable in disposition, and cordial and firm in his friendships."

LIST OF THE PASTORS

OF

THE CHURCH AT ALBANY.

Rev. Johannes Megapolensis,...........1642 to 1649,
" Gideon Schaats,..................1652 to 1683,
" —— Niewenhuysen,..............1675 to ——,
" Godfreidus Dellius,...............1683 to 1699,
" Johannes Petrus Nucella,.........1699 to 1702,
" Johannes Lydius,.................1703 to 1709,
" Petrus Van Driessen,.............1712 to 1739,
" Cornelius Van Schie,..............1733 to 1744,
" Theodorus Frelinghuysen,.........1746 to 1760,
" Eilardus Westerlo,................1760 to 1790,
" John Bassett,.....................1787 to 1805,
" John B. Johnson,..................1796 to 1802,
" John M. Bradford,.................1805 to 1820,
" John DeWitt,......................1813 to 1815,
" John Ludlow,......................1823 to 1833,
" Thomas E. Vermilye,..............1835 to 1839,
" Duncan Kennedy,...................1841 to 1855,
" Ebenezer P. Rogers,..............1856.

OFFICERS OF THE CHURCH,

FOR 1858.

Pastor,

REV. EBENEZER P. ROGERS, D. D.

Elders,

John Q. Wilson, Stephen Van Rensselaer,*
Philip Ford, Edmund S. Herrick.†

Deacons,

David Newland, Maurice E. Viele,‡
Edward Dunscomb, William Seymour.§

Trustees,

Jacob H. Ten Eyck, Alfred Van Santvoord,
Peter Gansevoort, John H. Reynolds,
Lansing Pruyn, Henry Lansing,
Robert H. Pruyn, S. Oakley Vanderpoel,
Henry T. Buell.

Treasurer,

Richard Van Rensselaer.

* In place of Wm. McElroy, Elder, 1856-7.
† do Timothy Seymour, do.
‡ do Jacob J. DeForest, Deacon, 1856-7.
§ do David McMicken, do.

AN ACT

IN RELATION TO THE MINISTER, ELDERS AND DEACONS OF THE REFORMED PROTESTANT DUTCH CHURCH IN THE CITY OF ALBANY.

Passed February 4th, 1857.

The People of the State of New York, represented in Senate and Assembly, do enact as follows:

SECTION 1. The corporation known as the minister, elders and deacons of the Reformed Protestant Dutch Church in the City of Albany, shall hereafter be known and styled as the Reformed Protestant Dutch Church of the City of Albany.

§ 2. The proceedings of said Church, pursuant to the provisions of chapter ninety, of the laws of eighteen hundred and thirty-five, entitled "An act to amend the charter of the minister, elders and deacons of the Second Protestant Reformed Dutch Church in the City of Albany," to vest the property of said corporation in a board of trustees, are hereby confirmed.

§ 3. Jacob H. Ten Eyck, Peter Gansevoort, Robert H. Pruyn, John H. Reynolds, Lansing Pruyn, Alfred Van Sanford, S. Oakley Vanderpoel, S. Visscher Talcott, Henry S. Lansing, the trustees of said Church, elected in the month of January, one thousand eight hundred and fifty-six, are hereby declared to be the first trustees of said corporation, to hold their offices for the term of one, two and three years, from the first Monday of March, one thousand eight hundred and fifty-six, agreeably to the classification into three classes made immediately after their said election, in pursuance of law.

And on the first Monday of March, in each and every year, an election shall be held for three trustees of said corporation, in place of those whose term shall then expire, and at the same time to fill any vacancies which may not have been filled by said trustees, and also elect three inspectors of election. At least one week's notice of the time and place of holding said election shall be given by notice from the pulpit of said Church, or by affixing a written notice on the outer door thereof. Said trustees shall appoint three persons to hold said election on the first Monday of March next, and shall have power to fill any vacancies which may exist thereafter, for any reason whatever. And in the event of such election not being held in any year, the trustees whose term shall expire in that year, shall hold office until their successors shall be elected, and it shall be the duty of the trustees, within three months thereafter, to fix the time and place of holding said election, and to give notice thereof as aforesaid.

§ 4. The Reformed Protestant Dutch Church of the City of Albany shall be entitled to receive and collect all rents reserved in and by any and all leases of pews in the Church, belonging to said corporation, heretofore made by the minister, elders and deacons of the Reformed Protestant Dutch Church in the City of Albany, as fully as if their corporate name had not been changed as hereinbefore provided.

§ 5. But nothing herein shall be construed to affect any action now pending in favor of or against the said corporation; and in case any suit shall be hereafter commenced against the said corporation in this state, or elsewhere, by any person or party not knowing the change of the corporate name of said corporation, it shall not be authorized to plead a misnomer, but shall answer or plead to the merits of the action, stating in such answer the true name of said corporation; and such action shall proceed against it, in either name, according to the practice of the court in which such action shall be pending; and any judgment recovered therein shall be as valid as if the action had been commenced and conducted against the said corporation by its true name.

§ 6. This act shall take effect immediately.

www.ingramcontent.com/pod-product-compliance
Lightning Source LLC
LaVergne TN
LVHW021415110826
845150LV00007B/1933

* 9 7 8 1 4 2 5 5 1 0 1 4 5 *